Professional Values and Practice

Also available

Learning and Teaching
The Essential Guide for Higher Level Teaching Assistants
Anne Watkinson
1-84312-251-0

The Essential Guide for Experienced Teaching Assistants
Meeting the National Occupational Standards at Level 3
Anne Watkinson
1-84312-009-7

The Essential Guide for Competent Teaching Assistants
Meeting the National Occupational Standards at Level 2
Anne Watkinson
1-84312-008-9

Assisting Learning and Supporting Teaching
A Practical Guide for the Teaching Assistant in the Classroom
Anne Watkinson
1-85346-794-4

Professional Values and Practice

ANNE WATKINSON

David Fulton Publishers

David Fulton Publishers Ltd
The Chiswick Centre, 414 Chiswick High Road, London W4 5TF

www.fultonpublishers.co.uk

David Fulton Publishers is a division of Granada Learning Limited, part of ITV plc.

Copyright © Anne Watkinson 2005

British Library Cataloguing in Publication Data
A catalogue record for this book is available from the British Library.

ISBN: 1 84312 250 2

10 9 8 7 6 5 4 3 2 1

Typeset by RefineCatch Limited, Bungay, Suffolk
Printed and bound in Great Britain

Contents

Preface

This is an exciting time for teaching assistants (TAs). Your role in supporting and promoting the learning and teaching of all children and young people is being accompanied by considerable funding for development and recognition. There are a lot of different levels you can now work at, depending on your own abilities and the needs of your school. The role has been compared with that of nurses working alongside doctors – a complementary addition to the teaching staff of a school.

The recognition of the various levels has brought about a whole host of training programmes for TAs: induction training, National Occupational Standards at levels 2 and 3; and now standards at a higher level have been published by the Teacher Training Agency. This book is aimed at those TAs who either are being appointed at Higher Level Teaching Assistant (HLTA) level or who are working towards HLTA status recognition. HLTAs, by the very nature of the expectations surrounding the role, should be able to read widely, consult and discuss issues with school colleagues.

This book should stimulate thought and action, promote discussion and create opportunities for reflection – key skills for HLTAs. This particular volume aims to deal with the underlying philosophy and principles of practice; a companion volume is also available* which deals with the more practical aspects of the teaching and learning part of the HLTA role. Both books are needed to underpin your HLTA status and to get you thinking about the generic issues of the role, but you will need to read further to cover specific curriculum or special needs aspects.

* *Learning and Teaching : The Essential Guide for Higher Level Teaching Assistants* by Anne Watkinson, 2005, David Fulton Publishers.

Acknowledgements

I would like to thank:

- The schools, LEA advisers and colleagues with whom I have discussed the many issues that this initiative raises.

- The staff of schools who have been so willing to spend time with me and tell me about their successes and attempts at making sense of the school workforce remodelling intentions and practicalities.

- The staff, children and parents of Hinguar Community Primary School, the staff of St Luke's Primary School, Tiptree, and the staff of Essex Wildlife Centre for permission to use the photographs included.

- Clacton High School for permission to include some pages from their TA Career Development Portfolio.

- The many schools and TAs, whose practice and friendship has been a constant inspiration throughout my work with them.

- Margaret Marriott of David Fulton Publishers for her continuing positive feedback and help while preparing the book.

- My husband Frank, for his endless patience, domestic help and support with my ICT systems.

Abbreviations

ASE	Association for Science Education
DfES	Department for Education and Skills
EBD	Emotional and behavioural difficulties
FE	Further education
G&T	Gifted and talented
GTC	General Teaching Council
HE	Higher education
HLTA	Higher Level Teaching Assistant
ICT	Information and communication technology
IEP	Individual education plan
INSET	In-service education for teachers
LEA	Local Education Authority
LSA	Learning Support Assistant
NC	National Curriculum
NOS	National Occupational Standards
NVQ	National Vocational Qualification
Ofsted	Office for Standards in Education
PPA	Planning, preparation and assessment
QCA	Qualifications and Curriculum Authority
QTS	Qualified Teacher Status
SAT	Standard Assessment Task or Test
SDP	School Development Plan
SDT	Senior Designated Teacher
Sebs	Social, emotional and behavioural skills
SEN	Special Educational Needs
SENCO	Special Educational Needs Coordinator
TA	Teaching Assistant
TTA	Teacher Training Agency

Introduction

Background

The Higher Level Teaching Assistant (HLTA) status is part of the government's larger reform of the school workforce which aims to raise standards and tackle teachers' workload (DfES/TTA 2003a). The intention is that extra support staff, both inside and outside the classroom, will help teachers focus on their teaching role and provide more support for pupils' learning so that higher standards can be achieved in the future. For you it means that you are able to go one step higher in the membership of a recognised profession. Your role is no longer invisible; people are proud to say they are teaching assistants, and non-educationalists understand some of the importance of your role.

For the first time you have something like a career ladder. Four levels have been agreed which fit into the national qualifications framework, HLTA status being in the highest level. National Occupational Standards (NOS) for level 2 and level 3 have been written (LGNTO 2001). HLTA standards have been drawn up by the Teacher Training Agency (TTA) (DfES/TTA 2003). The courses associated with these standards, along with the Department for Education and Skills (DfES) Induction Training for TAs, foundation degrees for TAs and the HLTA developments, mean that there is a framework of training associated with the career levels which is nationally available and recognised.

Awarding bodies have been busy drawing up courses to match the NOS, so that TAs can get national recognition for training. The DfES induction training is matched to the NOS, so that undertaking it can be credited where feasible. National Vocational Qualifications (NVQs) for TAs have been established for a year or so, and are recognised throughout Great Britain. The routes to achieving HLTA status are described in more detail in Chapter 7. There are various further (FE) and higher education (HE) colleges, LEAs and other course providers who are busy setting up systems and resources to teach all courses.

There is just one word of warning: HLTA status, if awarded, is not a qualification, it is a recognition of your competence and abilities to do the job. While it is considered that people acquiring this status will be operating at the equivalent of a second year degree level, it does not replace such a qualification. If you want to go on to be a teacher you will still have to undertake a full degree course in a chosen subject before qualified teacher status can be considered. The acquisition of the HLTA status could, however, provide evidence to any HE college of your experience, interest in education and level of competence.

Table 1.1   The possible range of tasks and levels for TAs in schools

Level	Job profile summary (NJC 2003)	Training, status recognition and qualifications available
Induction/basic skills	Working under direction/instruction Supporting access to learning • welfare/personal care • small groups/one to one • general clerical/organisational support for teacher	DfES Induction training available through LEAs Some mapping to levels 2 and 3 available (see EO or teachernet website)
Level 2	Working under instruction/guidance Enabling access to learning • welfare/personal support – SEN • delivery of pre-determined learning/care/support programmes • implement literacy/numeracy programmes • assist with planning cycle • clerical/admin support for teacher/department	English and mathematics awards (see Annex B TTA 2004:40) NVQs and related qualifications (see EO 2004:9) based on the NOS level 2
Level 3	Working under guidance Delivering learning • involvement in whole planning cycle • implement work programmes • evaluation and record keeping • cover supervisor • specialist SEN/subject/other support	NVQs and related qualifications (see EO 2004:9) based on the NOS level 3 Modern apprenticeships for the under 25s
Behaviour/guidance/ support	• pastoral support • learning mentors • behaviour support • exclusions, attendance	
Level 4	Working under an agreed system of supervision/Management delivering learning Specialist knowledge resource • lead planning cycle under supervision • delivering lessons to groups/whole class • management of other staff	HLTA status (NOT a qualification) TA foundation degrees Possible level 4 NVQ in future
Behaviour/guidance/ support	Manage systems/procedures/policy • pastoral support • mentoring/counselling • behaviour • exclusions, attendance	

| Qualified teacher status | Responsible for teaching and learning of group of pupils, Education Act 1998 (2003)
a planning and preparing lesson and courses for pupils
b delivering lessons to pupils (including via distance learning or computer aided techniques)
c assessing the development, progress and attainment of pupils; and
d reporting on the development, progress and attainment of pupils | Graduate status plus postgraduate teaching certificate Degree including qualified teacher status |

Support through reading

This book is one of a series I have written supporting the various levels of TA development. Whatever stage you are at in your career path as a TA, you have continuing professional development needs. Reading and reflection are part of this process. The first three books in the series help TAs develop their thoughts at the various lower levels of the standards. The first, *Assisting Learning and Supporting Teaching*, was written to give some background after the introduction of the induction training materials (Watkinson 2002). The other two were written to support those TAs undertaking qualifications or wanting background reading when working at levels 2 and 3. These were called *The Essential Guide for Competent Teaching Assistants* and *The Essential Guide for Experienced Teaching Assistants*, respectively (Watkinson 2003a; 2003b).

This book is one of a pair being written to support the acquisition of the HLTA standards. They will not provide the detailed information you need for curriculum subject knowledge and understanding. They are not intended to help you with understanding the specific special educational needs (SEN) of individual pupils. They will not therefore cover all the standards. Standards 2.1, 2.2, 2.3, 2.4, 2.6, and 2.8 will all require more detailed study than either of these generic books will provide. This is important to remember, as to gain the award you have to show that you fulfil *all* of the standards. They are seen as an holistic set, not a set from which you can pick and choose, as with the NVQs.

The books are about the generic issues which underpin all that you do as an HLTA, regardless of whether you are specialising in a particular subject or SEN at whatever key stage you work in. This book deals largely with the standards, values and principles that underpin the practice of learning and teaching. The contents of the books will hold good whatever the subject matter being taught or whoever is teaching. The second book covers the putting of those principles into practice, again in a generic way. The books are not courses in themselves, nor do they pretend to provide the last word in the area. You need to meet, exchange views and see examples of good practice, find out about the latest resources and keep abreast of new ideas in education, teaching and learning and about children and young people themselves. Above all you need to be working in a school, where all the staff take part in in-service education for teachers (INSET) activities, where you feel able to ask questions and where you can find support of various kinds.

It is essential that someone on the teaching staff takes a particular responsibility for the TAs in order that there can be in-house training and liaison over curriculum and pupil-related matters. Hopefully, if you are participating in any formal course, you will have a mentor. It is important for an HLTA that this is a teaching staff member, as you will need to learn about many of the activities of the teachers. You will be teaching classes, not acting as a cover supervisor. If you go for HLTA assessment, you will need a spokesperson teacher to talk with the assessor. It is possible that for the lower levels of TA, a more senior TA could be a suitable mentor.

No book or course can provide you with all you need to work as an HLTA; actual practice in schools must be both observed and experienced by you alongside the discussion with relevant staff about what and how things are done. All schools are different and have their own policies and procedures, both written and understood. The culture and ethos – the ways in which a learning atmosphere is created – are difficult to define in words. They can, however, be felt and observed. The legal requirements for schools all need to be backed by the school's interpretations of how these measures are observed in the particular building, or with the particular range of people and pupils who have contact with the school.

If you are not undertaking a formal course, it is hoped that the book and its companion volume will provide a useful reference for general use at the higher TA level. It is also important, at the higher level, that you read more widely, as a course textbook must be a basic text. The level of study for HLTAs is recommended to be at second year degree level. These books will give some recommended reading for you to dip into. Your local library will be able to get the books referred to, or some of the teachers may already have copies. There may even be a staffroom library, or you may live near a teacher training college that will have many relevant books.

Some of the books in such a library will seem rather theoretical and possibly difficult to read, but you should, at this level, be able to dip into books and seek out relevant passages or chapters fairly easily and will have, hopefully, a good grasp of most of the educational jargon. Librarians of such colleges can be a most valuable source of expertise and help you find books in the area of your particular interest. There is already a wide range of books available from David Fulton Publishers, already often used by those of you who support SEN, for conditions such as Asperger's Syndrome, Down's Syndrome, visual impairment, dyslexia, speech and language difficulties, gifted and talented, and so on. Do get hold of the latest catalogue from David Fulton Publishers and further information by using their website.

If this is the first time you have studied since leaving school, you are going to find some of the study hard. You need to consider whether you should undertake a short course in study skills. *Successful Study* (Ritchie and Thomas 2004) was particularly written with TAs in mind who are aiming to undertake a foundation degree. Ask at your local FE college what is available for returners to study. Some of the books being written to support foundation degrees for TAs will be of interest to you.

If you are considering whether to undertake the training, and how any existing qualifications and experience fit into the requirements, including the foundation degrees, or just reading this book, you will need both a copy of the standards (DfES and TTA 2003) and a copy of the TTA *Guidance to the Standards* (TTA 2004).

This book

This particular book of the generic pair will address the more intangible areas of your professionalism, and the principles and values which underpin so much of what happens in schools. Chapter 2 covers these within the umbrella of professionalism. Schools are organic living things, dealing with human beings, both adult and growing, who have feelings and needs. These must be considered before and alongside all the technical matters of curriculum and technique. Chapters 3 and 4 therefore deal with the relationships you need to consider with pupils and other adults. Chapters 5 and 6 address your legal obligations to the pupils in your care and your work colleagues. Chapter 5 looks at the context in which you work, the whole-school scene and the policies within which you work. The policies of the school will be their interpretation of how the law is to be upheld in the local situation. The importance of the school's ethos and culture is emphasised. As an HLTA, you should be taking a leadership role and considering influencing the formation of school policies. You are working in the school, becoming part of the establishment, ensuring you respond to consultations and attending appropriate meetings to voice your opinion.

Chapter 6 looks at the legalities through a national perspective. Central accountability, directives and initiatives have increasingly directly affected the way in which a school works. You cannot change the legal framework except, in a democratic society, by using your access to your MP to change laws through acts of parliament. Finally, Chapter 7 will give you pointers to the ways in which you can ensure your continued professional development within the education system. Your final career destination may not be within education but in one of the other caring professions such as medicine or social services. Becoming an HLTA is more clearly aimed at those of you wishing to make schools your long-term destination. Hopefully, for many of you, HLTA status will be the pinnacle of your aspirations, as Nurse Practitioner status is for nurses. But just as in medicine some nurses go on to be doctors, probably about 10 per cent of you will wish to use this training and experience to go on to be fully qualified teachers.

As with the level 2 and level 3 standards, many of the standards need to be cross-referenced. For instance, professional values and practice must hold through all the teaching and learning activities or they are pointless. I therefore choose to use a more holistic and apparently mixed approach than the standards can. By their nature they have to be a list. The NOS were also very detailed, and could be carefully referenced in the *Essential Guides*. The HLTA standards are much less specific and not so accessible to careful referencing. Reference will be made where appropriate. The numbers in square brackets indicate a reference to particular HLTA standards. Where some items were dealt with at length in the lower-level books, they will be not be repeated in this book, but page references to them are given. It is therefore assumed that, because you have access to these books or you have sufficient experience, you will have dealt with the issues concerned anyway.

The table above gives you a rough guide as to where to find some of the content in this book. The second book will deal more specifically with the section 2 and 3 HLTA standards.

Table 1.2   The general areas of this text relating to HLTA standards

Chapter	Relevant HLTA Standard	Pages
1 Introduction		1
2 Professionalism	1.1	9
Being a professional	1.1, 1.3	9
Personal values	1.3, 1.6	16
Inclusion	3.3.3	17
3 Relationships with pupils		21
General relationships	1.2	21
With pupils	3.3.5, 3.3.2, 3.1.2	22
individually	3.3.5	24
in groups	3.3.5	26
as a whole class	3.3.5, 3.3.4, 2.9	28
4 Relationships with adults	1.3	37
Own needs	1.3, 1.6	37
Relationships with others	1.4	39
Leading a team	3.3.6	45
With parents and carers	1.5	48
5 Context of the whole school	3.3.8	53
Policies and procedures	2.7, 2.8	54
Health, safety and security	3.3.8, 3.1.4	57
Whole school climate and ethos	3.3.7	61
Learning environment	2.9, 3.3.4	66
6 Local and national context	2.7 with 1.1	73
Local		75
National accountability and initiatives		77
International		86
7 Personal development	1.6	89
Observation, evaluation, discussion, reflection		89
Career development		98

There are examples of practice given throughout the book, but you may be able to add some of your own.

There are some reflective activities for you to undertake or discuss with a colleague and there is an additional reading list at the end of each chapter, a few items of which are essential for an aspiring HLTA, and some you can dip into as your interest leads you. Good reading!

Essential reading

DfES and TTA (2003) *Professional Standards for Higher Level Teaching Assistants.* London: Department for Education and Skills and the Teacher Training Agency.

TTA (2004) *Guidance to the Standards – Meeting the Professional Standards for the Award of Higher Level Teaching Assistant Status.* London: Teacher Training Agency.

Some further reading

Barrow, A. (2004) 'The changing educational scene', in Bold, C. (ed.) *Supporting Learning and Teaching*, pp. 14–33. London: David Fulton Publishers. A brief résumé of educational history giving background.

Cole, M. (ed.) (2002) *Professional Values and Practice for Teachers and Student Teachers,* 2nd edn. London: David Fulton Publishers. A reader of articles written by various authors to each of the standards for qualified teachers; worth dipping into.

Hayes, D. (2003) *Planning, Teaching and Class Management in Primary Schools,* 2nd edn, Chapter 8: 'Professional values and practice', pp. 117–132. London: David Fulton Publishers. A structured approach for trainee teachers.

O'Brien, T. and Garner, P. (2001) *Untold Stories – Learning Support Assistants and Their Work.* Stoke-on-Trent and Sterling: Trentham Books. A series of accounts of their practice by learning support assistants revealing the hidden and invisible work done by them over many years.

Pollard, A. (2002a) *Reflective Teaching – Effective and Evidence-Informed Professional Practice.* London and New York: Continuum. Try the introductory chapter of a weighty tome intended for practising teachers, pp. 4–25. There is much in this book to last you many years of study.

Pollard, A. (ed.) (2002b) *Readings for Reflective Teaching.* London and New York: Continuum. The first five readings supporting the above chapter. They are by Dewey, Schön, Berlack and Berlack, Osborn *et al.* and Tabachnick and Zeichner, all short extracts from longer works.

Smith, P. *et al.* (2004) 'The employment and deployment of teaching assistants' (LGA 5/04). Slough: National Foundation for Educational Research with the Local Government Association. A very recent survey of the work being done by TAs.

Useful websites

www.lg-employers.gov.uk
www.fultonpublishers.co.uk
www.remodelling.org
www.teachernet.gov.uk/teachingassistants
www.tta.gov.uk/hlta

CHAPTER 2

Professionalism

Being a professional

As an HLTA you will be a senior member of your profession and so have increased responsibilities, not just in your job description but in leadership and setting an example to other less senior members of staff. You will become more autonomous and be expected to act appropriately – independent of direction and immediate supervision, at the same time as becoming more accountable for those very actions and their outcomes.

In the past the word 'professional' has been associated particularly with doctors, lawyers and qualified teachers. Also, in the past, members of 'the professions', once qualified, were expected and trusted to do their jobs unsupervised and without needing any more training. This is not so now. All professionals, whether of the old 'professions' or anyone behaving professionally, are now expected both to keep up to date and to be accountable.

The greater responsibility you hold, the greater will be your accountability and your personal responsibility for your own professional development. As a person you probably want to be respected, but this means you must also earn respect in the way you behave towards other people. This means being considerate, treating others as you would wish to be treated, remembering simple things like good manners which provide the oil for the machinery of social intercourse. Do not promise what you cannot fulfil. Be punctual, acknowledge gifts and help, offer help where you can. Listen and contribute to discussions appropriately. Remember little things like birthdays, or times when people eat or work. Professionalism in a job is really just an extension of these attributes. It may mean being more conscientious in keeping an appointments diary, or making notes of jobs to do. It will mean ensuring you get your priorities right. Leave behind your home worries when you go to work.

Research into teacher professionalism has highlighted three different views (Silcock 2003):

- Academics saw teaching as an autonomous, intellectual and creative job.

- LEA advisers and inspectors saw professional teaching as skilled, effective practice.

- The teachers interviewed saw professionalism as an outcome of practical expertise developed in schools.

To these views I would add another:

● Personal fulfilment and a sense of responsibility for the development of the pupils being taught.

There are dilemmas which you must face when your experience, expertise and personal values conflict with legislation or with a directive from a member of staff more senior to you. At all points in your career you have had this dilemma, but as your responsibilities increase, you must articulate these to yourself, and keep the thoughts under review.

Consider the following:

1 You are asked to take a particular lesson. Your subject knowledge in this area is sketchy but you know the pupils well.

 Do you agree to do it?

 Does it make a difference if it is an emergency or whether it will be a regular event?

 If you agree, what particular preparation can you make?

 If you disagree, what can you do to be able to agree to in future?

 Should you prepare yourself to take any subject lesson with the age range you usually work with?

 Does it make a difference if practical work is involved, or the lesson is to be in a laboratory or gym?

2 You are convinced that certain pupils need a particular kind of support, and to repeat the exercises they did the previous week. The teacher directing you insists that the literacy strategy scheme of work demands the whole class moves on to a different topic, and that picking out a few pupils to repeat the work of last week will single them out as different.

 What do you do and say?

3 You are a mathematics graduate. The parents of a particular pupil wish their child to have extra tuition out of school and have asked you to be the tutor. They will pay you; you know the school's systems as well as having the theoretical expertise, and you have the time available. But, you know the school frowns on coaching. The teacher with whom you work closely has told you of the pushy nature of these parents and you know the child works hard in school, certainly achieving all he or she is capable of. You could do with the extra cash.

 What do you do?

4 You find a small child crying in a corridor and stop to enquire what is wrong. They are very distressed so you put your arm round them to comfort them and lead them to the school office and medical room. The next day you are summoned to the head's office and an irate parent greets you accompanied by the child. You are accused of child abuse by inappropriate touching. The description given of the event bears no resemblance to what happened.

 What do you do?

As you increase your responsibilities, so the dilemmas will increase. I would advise you to join some kind of professional association that will give you advice on legal and contractual obligations and help you understand your rights and entitlements. Most teachers go through their professional career without problems, but it is helpful to know that if you are faced with contractual problems or are accused or abused yourself there are associations and unions that can help. As an ordinary TA, this is rarely a concern as you are so directed in your tasks, but the increased autonomy of HLTA status will bring with it increased risks. Being professional is not about 'toeing the line' but having an informed opinion which enables you to justify your actions, even if that means contradicting advice and direction. Some contacts are given at the end of this chapter.

The perception of the general public, and the media in particular, have mixed views about the professionalism of teachers and those who support them. You can be part of the effort to raise the public profile of teaching and TAs should be an example of what is valued in education. You have an opportunity to improve the image of your chosen profession as you will become more visible as an HLTA.

Professional values

The General Teaching Council (GTC) has developed a code of professional values and practice for teachers (GTC 2002). This organisation does not include HLTA membership, so until TAs have a professional body of their own, it is worth glancing at the GTC teachers' code. It points out that teachers have a strong sense of vocation. It is not just a question of competent classroom practice, but also of commitment, energy and enthusiasm in order to achieve success for the pupils. They also are in a constantly changing social situation. While working within the legislative framework, they need to challenge stereotypes, oppose prejudice, promote equality of opportunity, respect individuals regardless of gender, marital status, colour race, ethnicity, class, sexual orientation, disability and age. It is about having and wanting in others 'a spirit of intellectual enquiry, tolerance, honesty, fairness, patience, concern for other people and an appreciation of other backgrounds' (GTC 2002).

Consider the headings from the GTC Professionalism in practice and how they relate to your ideas on the professionalism of an HLTA:

Young people as pupils

Do you have insight into the learning needs of young people?

Do you have high expectations for them?

Do you demonstrate the characteristics you would wish to develop in the pupils you work with?

Teacher and support staff colleagues

Do you support and share with your colleagues?

Are you open to learning from others?

Do you respect others and maintain confidentiality where appropriate?

Other professionals, governors and interested people

Can you work in partnership with others, build relationships, respect and support them?

Parents and carers

Are you sensitive to the role and background of parents and carers?

Do you recognise their importance in supporting their children's learning?

The school in context

Do you understand the place of your school in the community?

Do you appreciate your own professional status within society?

Learning and development

Do you take responsibility for your own professional development?

Do you reflect upon your practice, continually hone your skills and deepen your knowledge?

Are you open to new ideas and technologies?

TAs are often positive people who do more than their job descriptions, giving considerable time in goodwill. All people who enjoy their jobs do this, but the implementation of the workforce remodelling exercise, releasing time for teachers must not depend on your good-will. There may be occasions in the near future, as the workload agreement is implemented, in some schools, where challenging situations arise. You could be asked to take on responsibilities either beyond that of which you feel capable, or the conditions of service or pay suggested seems wrong. You must decide where you stand, what you will undertake, when and under what conditions.

High expectations of pupils

The code of practice mentioned above and first standard of the new HLTA standards talks of having high expectations [1.1]. What is not defined is how high 'high' is, or what standard is to be considered as a benchmark and leaves the interpretation of this to the reader – or hopefully the school in which you work. HLTA standard 1.1 refers only to high expectations of pupils, not of personal HLTA behaviour, of colleagues or school procedures or of less tangible things like opportunities for development or integrity. It emphasises educational achievement. One can work in schools where the expectations of pupils to reach certain levels in examinations or tests is quite different from that in other schools geographically close. The guidance given by the TTA to support this standard is clear, indicating that an HLTA has to show all aspects of this standard in their work – expectations, the need to understand and respect the background from which your pupils come and educational achievement. The TTA give examples of how HLTAs can demonstrate this standard.

You must always try to set standards with the pupils with whom you work which get them to aim a little higher [1.1]. The word 'target' has become associated with test results and statistical outcomes. The original meaning, the analogy to archery, indicates that one can control the aim and should practise to perfect it. One can then reach a more acceptable place on the target, which has not changed. Changing the aim is especially important when working with pupils with low self-esteem, which is often apparent in pupils with SEN, pupils from home backgrounds with low expectations, or pupils who may have had poor previous educational experiences. Teachers' attitudes can affect those of the pupils. There needs to be a culture of high expectations throughout school life. This means throughout the curriculum, in sport, performing arts, practical and vocational subjects not just the more academic subjects. You need to be positive in informal times, and not unwittingly use 'put downs'. These can affect pupils' self-esteem just as allocation to a lower set can establish a view of achievement which is false.

Standards 1.2 and 1.3 give the ways in which you can overcome some of these barriers to success – by 'maintaining successful relationships with pupils' and demonstrating the 'positive values, attitudes and behaviour' you expect. So the ball is back in your court – it is up to you to have high expectations of yourself as well as the pupils!

Case study example

A teacher who had developed ways of working with both pupils and colleagues, including the use of an experienced TA was appointed to be an advanced skills teacher. Not only did this recognise her talents and expertise as a teacher in her own school, but carried with it the responsibility for giving sample lessons in other schools. She was sent to a school in a nearby town, but felt useless. The expectations of behaviour in the second school by the existing staff were much lower than those in her own school. She tried her usual behaviour management strategies, not talking until the pupils were quiet for instance to no avail. Finally, in order to get any of the lesson completed she had to accept a background level of chat, which was unacceptable in her own school. As a visiting teacher, she was powerless to try to change a school culture which was long established and unwritten. The expectations of examination results, attendance and other related matters were also higher in her own school. The background of the pupils in the two schools was similar in culture, ethnicity and religion. Both towns were commuter London towns, but the second had a long history of economic deprivation and local unemployment. Social expectations of parents in the two towns were very different and it is likely that parental expectations of behaviour and job prospects were also different.

Educational principles

You may already have thought these through and be clear about what you stand for and why you are entering a new phase in your career – that of an HLTA, but it is a good time to review your principles. We just accept some things 'as read' because our family background, culture, or experiences to date have established certain ways of thinking and behaving.

If you are to be responsible for getting pupils thinking, you must be clear in your own mind about what principles and values underpin your statements or actions. You may be challenging their ideas of right and wrong, or providing guidance on what can be acceptable in others in the circumstances of your particular school, community and environment. Some of your principles and values will relate to your own private life outside school, but some will impinge on your work. It is these that you need to concern yourself with at present, although your personal ethos is bound to influence your work-based one.

The following list is a selection taken from a consultation text put out by the DfES in 2003. It has some useful suggestions of core principles concerning teaching and learning which you can consider in your context. The authors suggested that these draft principles can be used for discussion to refine the principles and for exploring practical ways in which the principles can be applied. They hope for widespread support for the principles themselves. I have used ones below which relate to the more personal values.

First, try writing down what you think you stand for in education.

Looking at the list of principles you have written.

Where did they come from, why do you hold them?

Now look at the DfES list following:

Teaching and learning

Ensure every learner succeeds: set high expectations.

Build on what learners already know: structure and pace teaching so that they understand what is to be learnt and why.

Make learning of subjects and curriculum vivid and real.

Make learning an enjoyable and challenging experience: stimulate learning through matching teaching techniques and strategies to a range of learning styles and needs.

Develop learning skills and personal qualities across the curriculum inside and outside the classroom.

Use assessment for learning to make individuals partners in their learning.

School improvement

Focus systematically in the priority for improvement that is likely to have the greatest impact on teaching and learning.

Base all improvement activity on evidence – particular data about relative performance against benchmarks.

Build collective ownership through leadership development.
  (DfES 2003b)

Do the statements tally with what you expect of yourself?

Do they reflect your experience of school when you were a pupil?

Do they reflect the behaviour of the teachers and other staff around you?

Can they be held to all the time?

What might make a difference as to whether you can hold these principles?:

Can learning always be enjoyable?

Are there times when discomfort, making mistakes or being under some kind of stress can actually improve the speed with which things are learnt or its efficacy?

Is all assessment a process for the individual?
  (Isn't it often done to justify the action of the school or provide accountability for a person or institution?)

Can all activities be justified through the provision of evidence?

Are there times when gut feeling or intuition provide insights which cannot be proved?

Are these the only principles by which you would take action in school?

Educational values

'Education influences and reflects the values of society, and the kind of society we want to be. It is important therefore to recognise a broad set of common values and purposes which underpin the school curriculum and the work of schools'. (DfEE 1999a: 10; 1999b: 10)

This is a quotation from the introduction to the National Curriculum (NC). All TAs should read these introductory paragraphs, as well as the statement of values by the National Forum for Values in Education and the Community given at the end of both of the NC guides. The statements quoted cover the areas of self, relationships, society and the environment, valuing:

● ourselves as unique human beings capable of moral, spiritual, intellectual and physical growth and development;

● others for themselves, not only for what they have or what they can do for us;

● relationships as fundamental to the development and fulfilment of ourselves and others and the good of the community;

- truth, freedom, justice, human rights, the rule of law and collective effort for the common good;

- families as sources of love and support for all their members, and as the basis of a society in which people care for others;

- the environment, both natural and shaped by humanity, as the basis of life and source of wonder and inspiration. (DfEE 1999a: 148,149; 1999b: 196,197)

The DfES has recently sponsored a project that teaches positive concepts to children from the age of five. It was not about promoting any one religious tradition, or style of curriculum but about establishing a moral atmosphere helping students become better people. One outcome of the project is a most helpful booklet on *Values Education*. The main features were:

- a set of universal values central to how the school works and adults and children conduct themselves and relate to each other;

- explicit consideration, both in assemblies and in specific lessons, of what these values mean, focusing on one each month, based on a cycle of twenty-two values over a two-year period;

- an expectation that all staff model positive values and behaviour to develop a calm and reflective learning environment;

- the use of reflection and visualisation to enable people to control their responses to external events by their internal processes. (Eaude 2004: 1)

Personal values

In terms of personal values, you may have thought these out carefully or never really considered them, just accepted that there are moral rules by which you lead your life. For some people these will be the Jewish and Christian Ten Commandments, for some the precepts of the Koran, and others the teachings of their own particular faith. We live in an increasingly secular world where the acquisition of material goods or money or fame are considered to be important. It is unlikely, if you have experience of being a TA or aim to enter the teaching profession that these latter will be the foundation of your reasoning. You are more likely to be wanting to work with children or young people, support pupils with learning difficulties, or trying for a job which enables you to fit in with your family life than seeking fame and fortune.

Your personal values are the bedrock on which you lead your life. They give you integrity and consistency which enable others to know where they stand with you and enable you to make decisions based on them rather than randomly or indecisively.

Do give yourself some time to consider your personal values separately from the principles or values which may be associated with working in a school.

Consider:　your religious or spiritual beliefs

your loyalties to your family and friends;

your need for personal space or a mentor or both;

your physical needs to maintain a healthy life;

your mental and emotional needs to enable you to function effectively.

Do you need time out to read or take part in leisure pursuits?

Where would you draw the line between voluntary and paid work?

What things would you not do if asked, regardless of financial or other reward?

How do you balance these various values with each other?

Case study

A TA was asked to undertake more hours (paid) to support a child with cerebral palsy. She got to know the mother well as she came to school to collect the child each day. As they got talking it turned out the father had found having a child with an obvious disability hard to take. He could not go with his child to public places, and his hang-ups finally led to separation from his wife and child. The mother talked at length to the TA about the problems this caused, both emotionally and physically. She asked the TA to come to her house as a friend. The TA also had a daughter who was a slow learner and sympathised readily with the pupil's mother. However, the befriending became more and more demanding, resulting in phone calls late at night and contact made during school time when the TA was with other pupils. The TA had to discuss the situation with her husband and with her line manager. Her wish to help and support had conflicted both with the needs of her own family and the needs of the job for which she was employed. Other counselling and social services support was found for the mother and her cerebral palsy child.

Inclusion

One of the principles that has determined educational policy at government and school level in the past decade has been inclusion [3.3.3]. The principle has developed from that of an understanding of human rights and equality which developed over the last few centuries in western cultures. The fight for votes for all, for a more equal distribution of wealth, the growth of movements like socialism and communism all came from a desire to see all people treated in a fairer way. Inclusion means more than equality of opportunity [3.3.7]. One of the difficulties of teaching, maybe the main one, is that we are all different, and all pupils are different. So the need to be 'fair' is not necessarily the most helpful one for all pupils.

It does not work just to ensure that all children go to school for the same length of time and take part in the same lessons. Organisation or reorganisation of systems is not enough to enable all children to progress according to their ability and needs. Teaching aimed at the middle of the ability range neglects those with higher or lower abilities. Those with physical or learning problems need support, hence the emphasis on what is now called SEN. Pupils with higher abilities need stetching or pointing in alternative directions to add more dimensions to their learning, hence the additional provisions for gifted and talented pupils. You may well be working with such pupils. Sometimes, TAs are asked to work with the more able children who need encouragement or adult support for an activity. Traditionally, however, your role has been to support those who are less able.

Until fairly recently pupils with learning difficulties or disabilities that impeded their access to teaching in a mainstream school were described as educationally handicapped. As such they were considered to require education in special schools that offered a modified curriculum that was different from that taught in mainstream schools, or requiring educating in schools that had specialist staff and equipment. The two kinds of school coexisted in most education authorities: mainstream schools which the majority attended; and special schools which catered for a minority of pupils with learning difficulties or physical and sensory disabilities. Since the implementation of the Education Act 1981 this picture has been changing gradually. Although special schools continue to provide for a section of the school population, an increasing number of pupils with significant learning difficulties or physical and sensory disabilities are being educated in mainstream schools. This is described as *inclusion*.

Until 1990 the term 'inclusion' had not been in common use in education. 'Integration' was more commonly used to express the alternative to education that segregated a section of children from the mainstream. Segregation was seen to be undesirable for social reasons as well as for educational reasons. If one group is segregated from the rest of society there is a tendency for them to become second class or low priority even if that was not the original intention. SEN became low status within the education system. The limited curriculum in many special schools went unnoticed. This is no longer so, as the entitlement to the NC for all pupils became law, and inspection ensured that there was a much broader curriculum. For those of you working in such schools, you will understand the challenge that such requirements impose upon the staff, buildings and equipment as well as the demands it makes on pupils. For instance, provisions of practical scientific activities for pupils in wheelchairs, or with severe behavioural problems can present a headache for teacher and assistant alike, as well as a logistic nightmare for the building planners. Providing a breadth of curriculum expertise in schools with a small number of teaching staff can also be a problem in special schools as it is in small mainstream schools.

Inclusion also is not a concern about pupils who would otherwise be excluded, usually for extreme antisocial activity. Since the abolition of corporal punishment in state schools, this became the ultimate disciplinary sanction for such behaviour. There is an increasing use of pupils' referral units, where such pupils can remain on campus but have special support. You may be working in such a unit, or have been appointed to work alongside such pupils when they are in vulnerable situations.

The integration of increasing numbers of pupils with SEN or emotional or behavioural disturbance (EBD) into mainstream schools and classrooms with additional support is not necessarily the answer, either to the practical and logistic problems or the social ones. A deeper level is needed. This is expressed as 'inclusion' or 'belonging'. The inclusive classroom is not one where, for example the Down's child sits with a TA engaged in learning tasks that bear no relationship to the curriculum followed by the rest of the class. Inclusive classrooms should be communities that accommodate and value every member. Thus one of the teacher's primary goals is to make sure that all children are able to participate as fully as possible in the routines and rituals of the classroom culture. Special schools are still needed. They are able to provide those with very particular needs with an appropriate education. They may well be the school of choice for the child or their parents. They do not have to be isolated. They can be included in the wider community of a locality as a valued part of a group of schools.

While inclusive education of pupils is now an objective of public policy in the United Kingdom, it remains the subject of debate. A recent government strategy document called *Removing Barriers to Achievement* sets out their vision for the future (DfES 2004a). Change brings with it uncertainty and anxiety. It may also require an adjustment of values and a reframing of formerly held beliefs. The appointment of TAs in a school may be part of a strategy to increase the inclusive nature of a school. If so, your contribution to the strategy will be enhanced by an understanding of the theory of inclusive education.

Look out your school's policy on Inclusion – you may find it as part of the SEN policy, the behaviour management policy or the one for equal opportunities.

How wide is its philosophy?

What areas of school life does it cover?

Does the school's vision statement or aims reflect an inclusive approach to pupils, staff, parents and governors?

Discuss the issues with the SEN coordinator (SENCO).

Participation in the routines and rituals of the classroom culture includes taking part in, and sharing in, the curriculum and learning experiences of the class. It includes working collaboratively with other children and learning from them as well as with them. Learning in school is a social activity and it is important that the pupil with SEN or EBD is fully engaged in the social dimension of learning in the classroom and in the social life of the school as a whole. If the school is trying to support fully the theory of inclusion, you will be there, not to take the child aside while the teacher enables the other children to move on but to work with the teacher to intervene sensitively where support is required to enable them to engage in learning as an equal participant with his or her class peers.

It is not only pupils who need to feel included. You are most effective when you know yourself to be an integral and recognised part of the whole school team and approach your role as such, hence an emphasis in this book on relationships and teamwork. The next chapter is dedicated just to these areas. As an HLTA, you may well become a team leader and need to ensure that your attitude and behaviour to your team is as inclusive as you wish to be in the whole school team. Included TAs will not underestimate the value of their contribution to the ethos of the school: 'Where the assistants feel as included as these, the likelihood is that pupils they support will also feel they are fully included in the classroom and school learning environment'. (Balshaw and Farrell 2002: 101)

Essential reading

Introductory paragraphs as well as the statement of values by the National Forum for Values in Education in the National Curriculum for the age range with which you work.

Any school policies on inclusion, equal opportunities, anti-racism, harassment, anti-bullying.

The school's mission or vision statement or statement of aims and objectives (usually found in the School prospectus and the annual report).

Some further reading

Values and principles

Eaude, T. (2004) 'Values education: developing positive attitudes'. Birmingham: National Primary Trust with Oxfordshire County Council, in Pollard, A. (2002) *Reflective Teaching – Effective and Evidence-Informed Professional Practice*, pp. 89–96. London and New York: Continuum.

GTC (2002) *Code of Professional Values and Practice for Teachers* [www.gtce.org.uk/gtcinfo/code.asp]. General Teaching Council for England.

Orlick, S. (2004) 'The professional framework and professional values and practice', in Brooks, V., Abbott, I. and Bills, L. (eds) *Preparing to Teach in Secondary Schools*. Maidenhead and New York: Open University Press.

Inclusion

Dip into:

Armstrong, F. *et al.* (eds) (2000) *Inclusive Education*. London: David Fulton Publishers.

DfES (2004a) *Removing Barriers to Achievement* (DfES/0117/2004). London: Department for Education and Skills.

Thomas, G. W. D. and Webb, J. (1998) *The Making of the Inclusive School*. London and New York: Routledge.

Some useful websites

Professional associations or unions being used by TAs:

www.unison.org.uk – a union for support staff

www.gmb.org.uk – a union for support staff

www.pat.org.uk – Professionals Allied to Teaching (PAtT): accessible via the Professional Association of Teachers (PAT)

www.napta.org.uk – an association formed by the Pearson Publishing group to provide services to TAs

The main teachers' associations:

National Association of Teachers (NUT) www.teachers.org.uk

Association of Teachers and Lecturers (ATL) www.teacherxpress.com

National Association of Schoolmasters and Union of Women Teachers (NASUWT) www.nasuwt.org.uk

CHAPTER 3

Relationships with pupils

General relationships

The HLTA standards are packed with references to relationships. Standard 1.2 refers to having good relationships with pupils, but this must be taken in conjunction with standard 3.3.5, where the HLTA is expected not just to work with individuals or groups of pupils but also whole classes. This opens up the necessity for a different set of skills. Communication at all levels is essential in any relationship, but spelt out for pupils in 3.3.2. Standard 1.4 refers to *working collaboratively*, 1.5 to *liaising sensitively*, 3.1.2 to *feedback*, 3.3.6 to *guiding others*, all activities dependent on relationships between people.

Effective relationships are helped by:

- A mutual accountability, whether doing the asking or being asked to complete a task of some kind.
- Mutual trust.
- Qualities like punctuality, truthfulness, honesty, and reliability building up the necessary trust.
- A recognition of your own mistakes – apologise and learn from them.
- Effective communication. This not only means listening, but also giving clear, appropriate and if possible unambiguous instructions or messages, even simple things like not mumbling when in doubt will help.
- Being explicit (politely) about needs and misunderstandings, implicit messages can be misunderstood, causing hurt or delay. Write things down for yourself and others where you can, being as accurate and concise as possible.
- Assertiveness without aggression.
- Positive attitudes such as trying to see the good in people or pupils, trying to understand, smiling where you can; for instance ask for things or give instructions in a positive not a negative manner.
- Good manners – try to thank for things wherever possible, without being a 'creep'.
- Cooperation and collaboration rather than conflict – although this does not mean always agreeing with others.

- Avoidance of damaging conflict and unnecessary confrontation – aggression and attention seeking do not get the same results as cooperation.

- Shared problems, and not allowing thoughts to fester.

- Common aims, objectives or goals – such as in a fundraising group, or a group trying to put on a play, makes people recognise the importance of burying differences to 'get the show on the road'.

- Shared values or similar backgrounds.

- Frequency of contact, helping people to get to know each other better; what the common interests might be and what areas of potential disagreement there might be and therefore how to avoid them.

- A lack of cliques, where groups of people become inward looking and exclusive – thus where backgrounds and cultures are different it is important to understand where people are coming from, why they say or do certain things, and if possible to celebrate the differences.

- Celebrating differences – the ability to speak more than one language, cook different dishes, have a differing style of dress or home furnishing, read different books is something to be proud of, share or show an interest in. (Watkinson 2003b: 20, 21)

Relationships with pupils

One of the characteristics of the TAs that I have observed over the years, seems to be an innate ability to get on with pupils. It is the reason they enjoy the job and have in the past undertaken many more menial tasks and had little remuneration.

Pupils come to schools to learn, and the purpose of teachers and their supporting staff is to enable this to take place as effectively and efficiently as possible. There is a power relationship, partly a result of age difference, and the dependency of immature human beings on those older and supposed to be more mature. It is also partly due to the impact of a defined curriculum and all the associated accountabilities. As pupils usually outnumber the adults, the adults can feel threatened if they do not put themselves always in a commanding position. Adults have feelings, concerns and interests which influence the situation. This was highlighted in a report on discipline in schools. This report, although done some fifteen years ago will still be around in your school somewhere and is well worth reading. The comments on relationships in schools and the effect of the resulting climate for the pupils are robust and to the point. 'When a teacher sees behaviour, judges it to be unacceptable and intervenes to stop it, it is the relationship between that teacher and the pupil or pupils involved which will determine the success of that intervention. Yet that relationship is itself affected by outside influences' (Elton 1989). The relationships of that teacher to all the other members of the school community and their relationships to each other will influence how that teacher behaves. Standards 2.9 and 3.3.4 talk of establishing and contributing to a purposeful learning environment.

A golden rule to remember when things go wrong, when working with pupils, or your own children, is that it is the misdemeanour or bad behaviour that you do not like, not the child. The young person must retain their self-respect and self-esteem, and feel that you

Watch a teacher who gets on well with their classes:

Do they always teach the same way?

Do they respond to the mood of the class as well as continue their planned lesson?

Do they share in the discussions of the class?

Do they negotiate?

and they can still talk and work together after any 'telling off' or operation of sanctions which you might carry out. Other golden rules are about making time to listen, valuing and respecting. Be consistent. Be sympathetic, encouraging and caring when you can, challenge the young person to develop the things they are good at and to show their good personal qualities when they can. Don't put them down, or let them put each other down.

The following list was one which a group of advisers drew up to use with groups of teachers. The idea is that you can change all the negative put-downs – all ones heard in schools – to positive statements.

Cover the right hand column and try the exercise for yourself if you like, or you may have other alternative ideas than the ones suggested by teachers below.

THE HEALTH DEMOTING SCHOOL	THE HEALTH PROMOTING SCHOOL
Some put-downs overheard in school	**Some suggestions for alternatives**
This is the gypsy traveller girl; she's come because of the trouble. Free dinners. (Teacher to class)	Welcome, you must be Joanne, or do you like to be called Jo? We have been looking forward to you joining us. We'll sort out what is happening for lunch later on. We hope you will be happy here. Everyone this is Jo.
We'll get you a proper school jumper from lost property.	Don't worry about clothes, we can sort out uniform some other time.
Go Back! You've come through the wrong door.	I'll show you the door we usually use.
No! You can't go to the toilet now!	Of course you can go to the toilet. Thank you for telling me.
Don't put your coat on that peg.	Can you remember which coat peg is yours?
Don't be stupid, do it like this.	Do you think that is helpful? Let's talk about other ways of doing this.
Where is your lunchbox? Did you bring it today?	(This depends on tone of voice rather than actual words.)

Your sister was never like this.	How is your brother getting on?
Put it over *there* – no! Not there – there!	Where do you think would be the best place to put it? Perhaps by my chair?
This is our part of the playground.	Do you want to join in our game?
You look stupid dressed like that.	You look smart today.
Don't come in here without your plimsolls – oh! yes your parents can't provide you with plimsolls.	Remember, it is plimsolls or bare feet in here.
Why don't you ever have what you need?	Let's check we have got everything we need.
Don't you have white shorts? Doesn't your mummy know to buy white ones?	Don't worry, the school provides team strip.
Wellingtons don't lose themselves. Where did you put them?	Can't you remember where you put your wellingtons? Have a thorough look and come back if you still cannot find them.
I need some big strong boys to lift this.	We need to move the tables – any offers?
You girls can tidy up.	Tidy up time everybody.
Boys, no splashing in the puddles.	Please avoid the puddles all of you.
You're wet? – Ugh – You're wet!!	Okay – we'll sort it out.

However positive and constructive you are with pupils, things will inevitably go wrong at some time. Don't worry about it; just try to think through how you could do it better next time.

Working with individual pupils

This can be at various levels and as an ordinary TA you will have experienced most of them. You may be in a totally physically caring situation, with a pupil who has a medical condition. You may be giving some learning support to a pupil who has missed some schooling and just needs to catch up, or a pupil with learning problems who can only cope in a one-to-one situation. This latter situation is becoming rarer as teachers become more adept at planning inclusive activities, realising that both the more able and the less able can, in the right circumstances, benefit by working together. Isolating a child for special attention immediately labels them as different.

There is a special area of school work, counselling, which needs proper training if it is to be fully effective. It can be time consuming and challenging. It is very valuable if the pupils come from family circumstances where no time is made for anyone to listen to their concerns. Potts has written a useful chapter on counselling and guidance in education (Potts 2004). She separates the two, and both of these from behaviour management. She believes that the three basic characteristics that will inform, enrich and enhance relationships between educationalists and students are the same as those required as the core conditions for a counselling relationship, namely *empathy, unconditional positive regard* and *congruence*. She also refers to emotional literacy – the understanding and practice of emotional intelligence. There will be more of this in the next chapter. She suggests the above characteristics are required, elaborating on each one and adds the skills of *active listening or attending, paraphrasing and summarising, prompting with clarification and open-ended questioning, immediacy and challenge.*

Take a few moments to reflect on your own experiences with individual children:

How often do you put words into their mouths or pre-empt what you thought they wanted?

How often did you do a task for them that given a bit more time they could have done on their own?

How often do you assume they understood when they did not?

How often did you have to rush – not because of the timetable but because you had become bored?

How often did you feel uncomfortable about what the pupil was saying?

To whom do you turn for help if you cannot deal with a situation or need more ideas?

Examples of good practice

One school decided that some of the children causing problems at playtime, did so as an attention-seeking ploy. They nominated one TA to be on duty at playtime, both in the morning and at lunchtime to be available just to listen and talk with the children who were causing trouble. Sometimes this support just meant there was someone with whom to isolate an offender. More often it meant that the TA became the person who listened to some of the troubles that the children were bringing to school from home, or it gave her an opportunity to discover the various sides in an argument.

A large secondary school saw such counselling opportunities as so important they paid for a trained counsellor to visit the school regularly. This person also trained some of the TAs in some of the methods he used so that they could continue his work when he was not present. Two of these TAs had gone on to take further training outside the school and were then delegated to run group discussion sessions with particular groups of pupils. This was a small group variation of circle time.

Just remember, that any relationship even with an individual pupil must be a professional one, warm, friendly, but not a substitute parent or 'buddy'. A close relationship does not mean you can forget your school's policies on child protection, confidentiality and health and safety [1.2, 2.7]. Also, you serve as role model in how you behave, which can be particularly

Photograph 3.1   A TA working closely with children encouraging their investigation

important if the pupil comes from a dysfunctional background or you are a different gender from the pupil's parent in a single parent family. This does not mean preaching in any shape or form. Respect for the pupil's background, their circumstances and culture, is vital.

Working with pupils in groups

When working with pupils more than one at a time, in group, class or informal situations, you have to consider not only your relationship with the pupils with whom you work, but also your facilitation of their relationships with each other [3.3.5]. Check all the items mentioned above in thinking about relationships in general and apply them to the pupils you work with.

Good relationships with pupils

Do you:

- listen to what they have to say?

- question them to explain more if you do not understand?
- try to see their point of view?
- give positive feedback and encouragement?
- facilitate their ability to contribute to a game or discussion?
- encourage them to cooperate when working in groups?
- explain rules and how they can be observed?
- ensure each one in a group can take part appropriately? That each has a turn?
- enable the pupils to recognise and learn from their mistakes without losing face?
- make goals, aims or targets explicit and praise when they are reached?
- look for similarities and celebrate differences?
- share joys and problems, yours and the pupils – establish rapport and understanding?
- look for opportunities to promote self-reliance, self-esteem and self-confidence?
- always show respect and good manners to all the pupils you work with?
- show a consistent and positive role model to the pupils in your relationships within the school?' (Watkinson 2003b: 25)

The above book also points out that you need to consider the age and stage of development of pupils regardless of their background. You should also consider where you are working with pupils, thinking about noise levels, space, comfort, even lighting. Elton found 'the behaviour of pupils in schools is influenced by almost every aspect of the way in which it is run and how it relates to the community it serves' (Elton 1989: 8).

Typical primary classrooms, with children grouped around tables in sixes look as though group work is a continual way of working when in fact much work is done in whole classes with the teacher talking or individually. The group members are often doing individual tasks, differentiated work on the same theme. This can often be seen in a literacy or mathematics lesson during the middle part of the lesson. Some readers may remember when teachers used an 'integrated day' approach, with several groups in the class engaged on different areas of the curriculum. They were encouraged to talk, but close observation showed the talk was often about last night's television not the task, as the task was an individual one, not a collaborative one. Collaborative or cooperative group work needs facilitating even training. The tables and chairs now found in most rooms can all be easily moved, and pupils, even quite young ones can be trained to move them themselves when different ways of working are called for.

Just as we feel the need to examine and practise the skills needed in good relationships, pupils need such help. The strategies which can be used to develop good relationships in a whole class will help groups within a class operate more effectively. The children have to be trained to work with each other within a group, share ideas, and work out problems. It is no good hoping the pupils will find their own way.

1   The grouping itself can affect the groups. You or the teacher may need to look at the distribution of dominant characters within the groups, or keeping apart those they know will antagonise each other. Groups need not be the same for different purposes.

2   The physical layout of the furniture by putting tables together, or the positioning of the group within the room can affect the way they work.

3   Teacher expectations of the outcomes need to be as high as for other kinds of work.

4   Ground rules for operating in the group need to be explained and explicit. They could even be written up in the classroom somewhere.

5   Roles within the group should be clear – who is leader or chairperson, who is scribe, who will fetch and carry in practical work.

6   The required end result must be clear – a group picture or model or one each on a shared theme? Will each pupil have to write up their own account or will a joint report be acceptable?

7   Groups need to be monitored to ensure as full participation as possible. Persistent disrupters need dealing with. The group must stay on task.

8   Timekeeping needs to be maintained on the groups' behalf, allowing time for recording results or scribing ideas, with reminders at appropriate points.

9   Once ways of working have become established pupils can be encouraged to experiment, negotiate, even to take risks in the ways they work together.

The NC, schemes of work and the recent strategies help make it clear where group work means collaborative work or just a way of organising differentiated work for various ability pupils. Choosing members of a group is important. There is evidence that mixed ability grouping, more difficult to plan for, does enhance the learning activity, whereas groups set by ability tend to reinforce the self-image of the group members, particularly those of the lower ability groups. Interestingly, British results show a greater spread of ability in any one age group when compared with those of other countries. Although our high fliers are among the highest in the world, and our average results come out favourably, we also have some of the lowest abilities in an age group. As part of your HLTA role will include whole class planning [3.1.1], you should be in a position to share your views on the grouping used by the class teacher as part of your contribution. Unfortunately, mixed ability teaching is not popular, as it is much more difficult to attain good results for all, especially with large classes.

Working with a whole class

This is probably the most daunting and contentious phrase in the whole of the standards for HLTA status. It has proved to be the stumbling block of the largest teacher union in signing up to the workload agreement, but it is also the one which carries the most responsibilities with it, just through the sheer consideration of numbers. There is a role of 'babysitting' a class which is now clearly defined. It is that of a cover supervisor. The HLTA not only has to 'babysit' a class, something possible with prepared work for the pupils already in progress, but has to *advance their learning* (my emphasis) [3.3.5]. This means you have to contribute to the teacher's planning [3.1.1], plan your own roles in the lesson [3.1.2], interest and motivate pupils [3.3.1], monitor pupils' responses and modify your approach accordingly [3.2.2], monitor pupil participation and progress and give constructive feedback [3.2.3]. As well as all this you must ensure that there is inclusion, equal opportunities, have concern for health and safety issues and so on.

So what, you may ask, is the difference between us and the teachers, apart from their salaries? Note the small print that ends all versions of the HLTA standards – 'Teaching and learning activities should take place under the direction and supervision (but not necessarily the presence of) a qualified teacher in accordance with arrangements made by the headteacher'. It is the teacher that carries the responsibility for the teaching even if it is carried out by you. The teachers are responsible for the learning of the pupils in their class – they are answerable to the school management, inspectors and accountable to parents for the whole experiences of those pupils. It is not about the act of teaching. TAs have always taught, even if it was only by example when cleaning up the paint pots or supervising the changing of shoes. Experienced TAs have always taught aspects of the curriculum as well as social skills.

One of the areas for social development that has tended to be ignored by teachers is the playground. Naturally enough, teachers have considered this time as their relaxation time, a time to avoid contact with pupils. TAs have increasingly been used as breaktime assistants, and many of you will also be doubling as midday assistants and so have seen for yourselves at first hand how the pupils behave to each other at this time. Some constructive work has gone on in some schools in training assistants to play games with the younger children and redesigning playgrounds [2.9 and 3.3.4]. The art of taking turns is being lost with the rise in solitary activities such as watching television and videos and using and playing with computers. Fewer families play card or board games. A playground marked out for hopscotch or chess can be ignored where children do not know how to play such games. Meals are no longer occasions to meet and talk in some families. Teacher training institutions have concentrated on curriculum knowledge and marginally on curriculum instruction, rarely offering help on developing social relationships in pupils. You are possibly in a stronger position than a newly qualified teacher, in having more experience in this area.

Many of you will have already learnt by experience and observation some of the techniques which teachers employ to maintain a calm working atmosphere in their class. Some of the ideas are just good practical tips, like sorting out how the furniture is arranged to enable discussion between the pupils or to facilitate a didactic presentation from the front. Some of these practical ideas will be explored further in the second book of the series. This chapter is more concerned with the often unspoken ways in which a teacher relates to the large group.

A strategy sometimes employed by schools is that of 'circle time'. This is not an easy option nor a different way of looking at the old infant 'newstime'. It needs to be carefully managed and facilitators, whether teachers, or other adults or, after experience, other pupils, need to be trained, especially in how to cope with potentially difficult situations. The work of Jenny Moseley in this area is well known. Pupils sitting in a circle taking it in turns to contribute on a subject does not just happen. The choice of subjects is important as well as the rules adopted by the group to ensure the way the time happens is useful and supportive to the pupils. The initial sessions need to agree on these rules, and sessions need to be regular. A sensitive leader will be aware of the issues that are affecting the group and know when to bring them up 'in public'. Sometimes an artefact is used to pass round the group to identify who is able to speak, this ensures only one person can speak at a time. Any member of the group can remain silent if they wish. Games can be part of the session time. They help the group with maintaining rules, taking turns and feeling part of the group activity. There has to be a health warning attached to such sessions though, as problems can be aired, or confidences shared which need dealing with carefully. Some children may find it difficult to communicate, and others could get carried away with what they want to say. Such activities need monitoring and may need supporting.

Consultation with pupils, listening to and valuing their opinions is now recognised as a most valuable way not only of understanding what the pupils really think but increasing their participation in their education as a whole. It makes a difference to the climate of the school, which makes a difference to the learning environment and the outcomes. A useful pamphlet has just been issued by the government (DfES 2004b) which outlines the benefits and principles of such an approach and offers some practical ideas of ways of proceeding – including things like circle time and school councils. The checklist gives items to consider and examples of what that would mean in practice.

The softer approaches

Pollard suggests that we need to adopt an interpretive approach – a 'working consensus' in the classroom. This is based on a mutual respect. Standard 1.2 clearly spells out this need for respect. 'Over a time, a good classroom relationship builds upon a store of shared experiences, jokes, anecdotes, and so on, which serve to ground classroom experiences. . . . However, a positive relationship, or working consensus, will not just appear. To a very great extent, the development and nature of this relationship will depend on initiatives made by teachers, as they try and establish rules and understandings of the ways they would like things to be in their classrooms' (Pollard 2002a: 118).

Any experienced teacher will tell you that the first few weeks or encounters are the most important in setting the scene. If you have watched teachers with a new class you will have seen how the children or young people may play a waiting game to see where the boundaries are, and then they try them out to see how far they can go with this new teacher. This can be particularly trying for supply teachers, unfamiliar with the 'norms' of a particular group. It will be particularly important for you as an HLTA, if you are to have a good relationship with a class, and enable their learning to progress, that you take note of these norms. One of the reasons for the success of TAs in taking over in emergencies is that they have consciously or subconsciously understood both the overt and the implicit 'rules' by which the class operates.

Cohen and colleagues, in their guide to teaching practice, list some points for trainee teachers when meeting their class for the first time (Cohen et al. 2004). You will be in a better position than the trainees as you will most likely know the school well and even the class. However, you will be in a different category, and some of the ideas might help. You will probably have the basic information about the class, but all the preplanning is important. Content, timing, presentation, beginnings and endings, transition between group work and whole class work can all be thought through beforehand. Try out some of their 'what ifs':

What will you do if:

- some equipment someone promised to lend you, or set out for you is not there or someone borrows something you were counting on to be in the room?

- the pupils work more slowly or quickly than you plan for?

- the pupils have not got pencils or rulers or other equipment you depend on?

- someone is late, needs to go in the middle to a music lesson, cracks a joke at your expense, mucks about?

- the class are not interested in something you thought would catch their imagination?

- you have a crisis of confidence?

- you lose your temper?

- you get preoccupied with organising and forget your lesson notes?

They also suggest considering what you wear, being firm but friendly, not trying to imitate certain mannerisms

One key factor is having something to say, having a secure knowledge base:

- knowing the pupils well, their learning characteristics, the individual needs, interests and foibles;

- knowing what you want to teach – the curriculum facts, the section of the scheme of work;

- knowing something about the teaching matter beyond what is put in the scheme of work – knowing the subject well;

- knowing about how children learn, the importance of motivation and challenge.

But none of this is enough without a relationship with the class. The secure knowledge base will give you the confidence you need to enjoy the pupils you are working with, give you a positive outlook and allow you to see more of their processes, to respect their points of view. This will form the foundation for your relationship with them.

Some other tips include trying to learn names as soon as possible if you do not already know them. Apologise if you make a mistake – we are all human. Offer to give help if someone is having difficulty, and the judicious use of praise and encouragement. Do not misinterpret the pupils' body language; avoiding your eye is not necessarily a sign of resentment, it could be fear of the unknown! Avoid overusing your power. Remember that golden rule: *criticise the behaviour not the pupil*. You can forget this in the heat of the moment and seem to 'pick' on a pupil, humiliate them, and attack them verbally. You will need to establish your authority fairly but formally at the beginning, set the working habits which you want to encourage; then when these are established, more informal relationships will develop. You will be able to trust the pupils to act responsibly and relate more as equals.

The skills required for working with pupils with SEN or those who are gifted and talented have been researched and result in similar lists; interestingly, a list which would

An example of good practice

An advanced skills teacher, working with a Year 9 class she knew well in a laboratory, with a TA also used to the class and was able to give out scalpels to cut plant material to take cuttings. On another occasion the same tool was used to peel a piece of fruit and chop it. There were 20 pupils in the class; they were a lower ability set in an urban comprehensive school. All the pupils knew, because they had been trained in using such tools, their potential dangers and their correct use. The norms of the school meant that no-one spoke when the teacher spoke. Instructions were followed, perhaps with a few reminders as to hurrying up. The teacher had established particular rules of behaviour for working in a laboratory from when the pupils first joined the school in Year 7. This meant all kinds of equipment and chemicals could be used, some potentially dangerous, some expensive and some needing particular skills. The pupils could be trusted. The two staff members could circulate confidently during the group work to help, encourage and support. Both staff members made sure they visited each group at sometime during the lesson. Pupils with poor motor skills were supported appropriately, both by the staff and by friends. The one or two isolates could work alone, but were also visited and their work commented on as the staff moved around. Prior to the lesson the teacher's planning would have included a risk assessment, but she knew the class well, established routines for equipment use, and she had no qualms about undertaking such a lesson. The pupils were able to move around freely, chat, joke both with each other and the staff. They knew the class and school rules and sanctions and had the reward of doing some interesting and challenging practical work.

be appropriate for all pupils! The list contains characteristics such as a sense of humour, enthusiasm, confidence, the knowledge base and flexibility. These will be reflected in an interest in the pupils' progress as you work with them. Success is not just a question of 'managing the curriculum', something that can be solved by adequate planning. Your skills and personality influence it.

Personalised learning

In an ideal world you would be able to give an equitable amount of time to all the pupils, to value their individual contributions [3.3.3]. Individualised learning sounds desirable, clearly if work can be planned individually for those with SEN, why not for everybody? In one lesson with 30 pupils, this is not only impossible, but inefficient. The recent publicity over personalised learning, as it is being called, is not a return to individual planning which took place in some early years classes during the height of the 'discovery learning' 'topic teaching' 'integrated day' incorrectly sometimes called the 'Plowden' era. It is not about one-to-one tuition. It is about allowing pupils to follow their choice of routes between certain options, all options having high standards in terms of teaching and learning strategies, assessment and feedback programmes which support pupils, school organisations which are flexible and include information and communication technology (ICT) options and partnership with parents and schools. It places an emphasis on dialogue, partnerships – relationships! It is about respect for pupils' ideas and providing equal opportunities [1.1 and 3.3.7].

There are ways in a simple lesson of making sure all pupils are consulted, feel valued and their needs are catered for. Provided you are careful with things like body language, for example getting eye contact in whole class sessions, grouping sensitively with appropriate monitoring, ensuring those with special needs are appropriately supported or challenged, you can remedy the time allocation over several lessons. Take care to talk with all the pupils at some time. Ensure you take in all work and monitor all work, and follow up those who are trying to avoid you. Attention to individual needs promotes good relationships and will result in fewer disruptive incidents.

There are, of course, times when your attention will need to be focused on individual pupils, enabling them to have special treatment. Any pupils new to the class will need extra support while they learn their way about, where to find things, the 'norms' of the class relationships, the policies and procedures which they should follow in class and in the school. They will be trying out a new set of boundaries. A pupil with a difficult situation at home such as a bereavement, or parents changing partners, a new baby, or a redundancy can all cause a change in the pupil's behaviour and learning patterns. Disruptive pupils are often attention seeking anyway, and do need to know that you will find time to be with those who are not disruptive. Most situations causing you to give extra time to certain pupils can be shared with the rest of the class, who may then also be able to give the pupil extra support and friendship outside the classroom.

Questions to ask yourself

Do you get on well with the pupils you have already worked with?

Are there particular characteristics which annoy you? What do you do about it?

Are you confident of working with pupils in large groups?

Do you know how you stand when you listen or whether you smile when you meet people?

Do you know what your voice sounds like when you are friendly or when you are angry?

Do you know what kind of questions you ask?

Do you think forming relationships is easy? Why?

If not, what do you find a problem? Can you talk with someone about this?

To whom will you turn if things go wrong?

The example reproduced on p. 34 of auditing your relationships with pupils comes from a secondary school's professional development portfolio – named by them a career development portfolio. You might find it useful to use.

Self-audit activity relationships with children

Aim To consider the factors that influence a good working relationship with children and to recognise where the relationship may need attention.

Instructions *Identify and tick the way that you work with children within the setting/classroom. Identify one of the four main ways in which you work in collaboration with the teacher.*

- Look at the examples of the indicators that could inform you how effectively you are developing your relationship with the children.
- Tick the examples in both columns, which apply to your situation: add any additional points of your own.
- Discuss with your mentor and or other teaching assistants to see how these influence your working relationship and what improvements can be made.

Children's attitudes to learning may alter from day to day and at different times of the day. Note inconsistencies so that they can be taken into account when planning.

A self-audit activity relationships with children
Teaching assistants work in partnership with practitioners/teachers in a variety of ways:

Think of a child with whom you work often.
Which of the following situations do you work in with that child?

1 Supporting in a whole class situation
2 In a group situation
3 Supporting on a one to one basis
4 Providing support to facilitate independent working and interaction

Working relationships may be going well if:	Working relationships may need attention if:
• The child is more relaxed	• The child is reluctant to play/work without TA's help
• The child makes positive contributions	• TA feels uncomfortable or anxious when working with a child
• The child comes to activities willingly	
• Tasks are usually completed	• The child finds it difficult to play/work in new or different settings
• The child and TA make decisions together	• The child is over familiar
• The child will become engaged in some activities independently	• The child is reluctant to work with TA
• The child talks to a friend about the activities	• The child is reluctant to use a range of strategies when unsure
• The child will ask others for help	• The child expects TA to solve problems and to take responsibility for the task
• The child seems to need TA's support less	• TA is unsure of role in supporting the child

Example 3.1 Two pages from the career development portfolio for teaching assistants at Clacton High School

Essential reading

Elton, R. (1989) *Discipline in Schools* (Report of the Committee of Enquiry). London: Department of Education and the Welsh Office. Still recommended reading after 15 years, and easy to read.

Any policy on behaviour management or teaching and learning which enables staff to provide a consistent approach to pupils and curriculum delivery.

Some further reading

Working with pupils

Leadbeater, C. (2004) *Learning About Personalisation: How Can We Put the Learner at the Heart of the Education System?* London: Department for Education and Skills in partnership with DEMOS and the National College for School Leadership.

Potts, S. (2004) 'Counselling and guidance in education', in Bold C., (ed.) *Supporting Learning and Teaching.* London: David Fulton Publishers.

Behaviour management

James, F. and Brownsword, K. (1994) *A Positive Approach.* Twickenham: Belair Publications Limited. Particularly useful at Key Stage 1.

Rogers, B. (1991) *You Know the Fair Rule.* Harlow: Longman.

Rogers, B. (2000) *Classroom Behaviour.* London, Thousand Oaks and New Delhi: Paul Chapman Publishing (Sage), Sage Publications Inc. and Sage Publications India Pvt Ltd.

Circle time – the original book

Mosley, J. (1993) *Turn Your School Round.* Wisbech: LDA.

Classroom management

O'Flynn, S., Kennedy, H. and Macgrath, M. (2003) *Get Their Attention! How to Gain the Respect of Students and Thrive as a Teacher.* London: David Fulton Publishers.

CHAPTER 4

Relationships with other adults in school

If you are working in a school as an HLTA you certainly won't be able to be a shrinking violet, working closely with one or two pupils, or one teacher. The HLTA role means not just being part of a working team but playing a much fuller role in the whole school life. Some schools, trying to balance their budget with the workload agreement of ensuring 10 per cent release or non-contact time for their teachers, have suggested just paying the TAs additional money for taking classes and effectively demoting them for the rest of the week. While this could assist their supply problems, it does not really address the intentions of the role. If you are to 'work collaboratively with colleagues' [1.4], liase with parents and carers [1.5], improve your practice through observation, evaluation and discussion [1.6], and contribute effectively in all the areas described in sections 2 and 3, you must be able to put all of yourself into that mode. This creates a much harder problem for the school management team in terms of expenditure and personnel management, but where it has taken place after consultation, it has shown major benefits. But you have to play your part.

Considering your own needs

My level 3 book for TAs (Watkinson 2003a) discussed how the formation of relationships is dependent on the way in which each person's interpersonal skills are able to develop. Some people seem gifted with a good interpersonal intelligence, a concept put forward in the ideas of multiple intelligences (Gardner 1983). These people are able to get on easily with others, while those with a less developed interpersonal intelligence may seem shy or retiring or find communicating difficult.

Following Gardner's lead, others have proposed other aspects of intelligence which they feel are important. There certainly are not seven fixed parameters under which we all operate, but identifying these aspects does give us a way of discussing a difficult area. There has been interest recently in the concept of emotional intelligence. Goleman suggests combining the interpersonal and intrapersonal intelligences of Gardner to form emotional intelligence, and which can then be expanded into five domains:

1 Knowing ones's emotions

2 Managing emotions

3 Motivating oneself

4 Recognising emotions in others

5 Handling relationships. (Goleman 1996)

He looks at social competence and incompetence – the abilities that underpin popularity, leadership and interpersonal effectiveness. He also believes, thankfully, that we can develop good habits and improve upon our capabilities in this area and remedy any lapses.

In the book *The Intelligent School* the authors take the idea of multiple intelligences to look at whole school issues and consider awareness of others connected with the ideas of interpersonal intelligence. They talk of managing emotions in oneself and others: 'Management with emotions involves the skill of using interpersonal and intrapersonal intelligence to motivate others ... demonstrating vision, self-belief and determination, putting the concerns of others first and encouraging others to persevere in the case of setbacks and frustrations ... It concerns, therefore, an understanding that you are what you do', that actions can have as much, if not more impact, than words alone. Sensitivity is at the heart of this aspect of EQ (emotional intelligence) (MacGilchrist *et al.* 2004: 131).

Some people describe these ideas as 'touchy-feely mumbo jumbo', but the DfES are taking them seriously. They have launched a pilot programme called 'Social, emotional and behavioural skills' (Sebs) to look at practice in 1250 schools in 25 LEAs (Hastings 2004). Any school which is involved in a healthy schools project will have already come across many of the ideas: the importance of feelings like anger, or depression in how one learns, of the relevance of considering self-esteem and so on.

Consider someone you know who seems popular and gets on well with different kinds of people.

Do they show their own emotions?

Do they talk about their own feelings?

Watch their body language as well as their speech patterns.

Listen to their tone of voice.

Are they consistent in their actions and speech regardless of others or do they change depending on their audience?

Are they able to listen as well as talk?

Goleman offers a caution. He points out that people who are very good at connecting with other people smoothly, reading their reactions and feelings, can lead and organise and handle disputes, are performers or actors. This can turn a person into saying one thing and meaning another, creating an impression, without being true to oneself. So, the intrapersonal intelligence, the ability to understand one's own needs and feelings has to go alongside, to balance the social skills with a personal integrity.

I have already suggested in Chapter 2, that you need to revisit your own values from time to time. Intrapersonal skills are about knowing oneself. You will find the importance of maintaining self-esteem for pupils often referred to in books on teaching and behaviour management, but we also have this need. You have strengths to offer and have achieved positive things. You have interesting ideas and experiences to share. But, you have to recognise that not everyone will like you and you are not an endless resource for others. Some of your thoughts and beliefs will be different from others. You do not have to go along with everything anyone else says. Your personal integrity matters. It is a question of where you draw the line between making a stand, compromising or changing what you do and say. Only you can establish this.

You need to know who you are and what you stand for, your own personal identity. This does not prevent you from being a full member of school teams, learning from or working with colleagues [1.4]. Each group or team within the school will have its own identity, depending partly on the purpose of the group and partly on the individuals within that group. It is also important that you uphold the ethos of the school and what it stands for, play your part in the whole school team. Clearly this could cause you some internal conflict if your values and that of the school do not coincide. For some people this conflict is too great. They take the only way out that they can see and either move to another job or just resign. Some less determined, or more deserving of the salary reduce their commitment to the job, become disillusioned, and shut themselves away from colleagues. Some conform for the sake of peace, and live a double standard. Hopefully, none of these will apply to you.

Your relationships with others

Hayes' *Handbook for Newly Qualified Teachers* has an audit for looking at your relationship with other adults. He suggests the following:

Exercise 9.1 Audit of your relationships with other adults

Use the following criteria to carry out a regular audit of your relationships with other
   adults. Use the bullet points beneath each criterion to guide your thinking.

Developing a right attitude by . . .

Being positive about life in general

- See situations in terms of 'half full' rather than 'half empty'
- Look beyond the immediate problem at the end product
- Keep failure and difficulties in perspective
- Resist the temptation to moan about trivial matters

Giving other people's ideas a chance

- Take a keen interest in what people say
- Stay open to new possibilities
- Adopt a neutral stance until the situation is clear
- Take time to reflect upon the merit of new ideas

Showing the right body language

- Maintain good eye contact
- Incline the head to indicate understanding
- Smile or look serious according to the issue
- Face the person directly

Expressing your viewpoint with tact

- Speak openly but courteously
- Acknowledge the merit of different opinions
- Allow for the fact that you may be mistaken
- Show that you are willing to learn from others

Empathising with colleagues

- Demonstrate genuine care by word and action
- Try hard to understand their position
- Ask sensitive questions to help unlock uncertainty
- Listen more than advise. (Hayes 2000)

Relationships with other staff

TAs in the past have often related to teachers through a process of osmosis, acting in response to unspoken codes, sometimes not even communicating verbally. As TAs have got more experienced, and teachers and managers more understanding of their potential, communication has improved. TAs have become part of the teaching team and those sensitive antennae, which served them well with pupils, have helped constructive relationships with adults to develop.

Before the days of inspection and monitoring, teachers sometimes seemed shy when 'performing' in front of others even having other adults helping them. This has largely gone with increased accountability. There may still be pockets of resistance among some teachers, who may dislike having others around when they are teaching or see extra pairs of hands as extra work. Most of you will now be in schools where the teachers are only too willing for you to share their burdens, and non-contact time.

The increased responsibilities which you are now being expected to undertake will not be possible if you find relating to adults difficult. You do need to be confident yet responsive to other's opinions and feelings, an effective team player with some leadership skills, sensitive to pupils' needs but aware of the demands of the curriculum, able to show initiative yet always operate under the directive of a qualified teacher.

Teachers and support staff are generally people with well-developed interpersonal skills. The affective domain of their working life is important to them – they care about other people and the pupils and relate well to them. You may have avoided the staffroom in the past, short of time or even felt a bit excluded, but it is important to the life of the school for more than rest and relaxation. There may be some staffrooms where support staff are unwelcome, but thankfully these are now few. Even where the sheer growth of numbers of people and space restrictions have made life more difficult, the need for informal professional exchanges is recognised as being worth the effort and often even expenditure.

Interestingly, in lively, forward looking schools, the staffrooms have a high level of talk about professional matters as well as chat about holidays, social events, television programmes. In schools causing concern the chat tends to predominate. Teachers can get tired, stressed, jealous, angry like any other person. There has been low morale in the teaching profession, and those who work with them, because of the public perception of their role, the increasing reports of violent incidents, increased accountability and the workload issues. This has not helped to provide a relaxed working atmosphere in schools particularly if there are causes for concern in an individual school. Ordinary social chat is safer. Professional matters are left to the formal meetings. Simmering beneath the surface can be a culture of jealousy, resentment, suspicion even fear. Such feelings, if based on inadequacy and incompetence, breed entrenched ways of working with resistance to change, resentment of outsider help and poor communication. Attitudes to the pupils become negative and the adults become poor role models for the pupils.

Ben-Peretz and Kupermitz describe the importance of staffrooms, or teachers' lounges as they call them. (Ben-Peretz and Kupermitz 1999) They have a model to describe the relationship between the teachers' views of their staffroom and student achievement. They hold that a positive social environment is characterised by:

● opportunities to escape stress and enjoy 'private time';

● positive perceptions of the workplace;

● opportunities for professional collaboration.

It can provide a positive influence on school life characterised by:

● being able to deal with their professional problems;

● developing educational activities;

● treatment of individual students.

They believe that a staffroom with a strong social function facilitates a high level of teacher professionalism.

The staffroom can have a non-threatening, unstressful atmosphere which will promote networking and help the creation of teams. There are also some staffrooms with cliques, but careful management of the geography of furniture or placement of the teapot can mix people up. Secondary schools or large primary schools may have split staffrooms, even split sites, comfort breaks being taken in year teams, or subject areas, but again sensitive managers seem to be able to find ways of encouraging networking. In this way, professional issues can interweave with social interaction. While as an HLTA, you will need much more formal planning time with individual teachers or specific teams, don't neglect the social side of the staffroom.

As a TA in the school you will already have established communication pathways, understand the ethos and have had good support from your colleagues as you have risen up the career ladder in the school. I labour this point because in your new role you will be in a much more influential position regarding other TAs and need to work even more closely with many of the teachers, uphold the ways of the school, follow the established policies an procedures. Your best way of dealing with working relationships where differences of opinion are likely is through open debate treating the other members of staff as equals, whether mature qualified teachers or raw, newly appointed, straight-from-school, classroom support assistants. Take opportunities for discussion and consultation seriously. Play your part and remember the ultimate aim of the school is to educate the pupils. Their needs should come first.

Being part of a team

You will be part of a whole school team, however large the school, a TA team, possibly an SEN team or subject team of mixed teachers TAs, technicians and others [1.4]. A set of people gathered together for a purpose can just be a group. To be a team means having positive relationships between the members of the group.

What is your team like?

Look at this list and check how you feel about it, and then discuss it with your mentor. Is there anything you two together can do to improve any ways of working in your school?

Teams are working well when:

- members are clear what needs to be done, the time-scale involved and who is to do what;
- members feel they have a unique contribution to make to the work of the team;
- mutual respect prevails among members;
- a climate of trust encourages the free expression of ideas, suggestions, doubts, reservations and fears;
- individual talents and skills are used effectively;
- members are able to discuss alternative approaches and solutions before taking decisions;
- there are established ways of working together which are supportive and efficient in the use of time;
- progress is checked regularly and members are clear about who they report to and when. (Hargreaves and Hopkins 1991: 137)

Working closely with a teacher

I have previously written at length about the partnership between a TA and the teacher of the class in terms of an ordinary TA, but the kind of relationships you will be developing now will be more than this. In the classroom, when working alongside the teacher, the partnership ideas clearly apply, but you are now going to be expected to be able to be more autonomous, show your initiative and be responsible for more of the work that goes on. But, you have to still work under the direction of a qualified teacher. It may seem restrictive, but it is only fair to the pupils and their parents to know who 'carries the can' and only fair to the teachers, to

Photograph 4.1 A teacher and TA discussing pupil outcomes following the teacher observation of the TA at work

recognise the strength of having three or four years' full time training and the extra expertise, knowledge and understanding that this brings. It is largely a question of maintaining good relationships, and defining or redefining the boundaries of how you work together.

There are also regulations governing this relationship which clarify the legal situation. Section 133 of these regulations, Education (Specified Work and registration) (England) 2003, talk about the circumstances under which certain kinds of school staff other than qualified teachers, can carry out 'specified work' relating to teaching and learning. This covers planning, preparing and delivering lessons, assessing and reporting on the development of progress and attainment of pupils. All this has to be done in order to assist or support the work of a teacher in the school. The head teacher must be satisfied that you have the skills, expertise and experience to do the job. And you are *subject to the direction and supervision of a teacher* in accordance with arrangements made by the head teacher of the school. You must be clear what these arrangements are and have spoken with the teacher or teachers concerned about how this will work in practice. Any preliminary time spent on clarifying your future working relationships will pay dividends when you are both under pressure to get things done, or get tired or need extra support.

Some teachers you will like and respect with no trouble, others you may find more difficult. Just remember your professionalism. Do not let your feelings show. Work on the positive things in your relationship, and – you never know – you may get to like them! Working with them, relating to them may reveal reasons for their standoffishness, or sadness or whatever annoys you. With understanding will come a greater ability to work together. Your support may actually be just what they need and they have not recognised it.

With other members of the school community

Governors should be monitoring the activities of the school, to see that all staff including the head are carrying out the things agreed in the school development plan (SDP) – another document they should be instrumental in drawing up, but are often appearing just to rubber stamp. Active governing bodies work in partnership with the school and there is a seamless interchange of information. You may be monitored by the governors, as they will have agreed to your appointment and training. As a new kind of appointment they will be particularly interested in how the new ideas will work in practice. Do talk with them and feel you can be open with them about your views and welcome their interest if they want to observe your work in action. If you are a governor, remember there are times when your professional role will exclude you from certain activities, like serving on some of the appointment committees.

You may even be on the governing body, where other staff have seen you as a good representative of their views and you have the time to commit to such activities. While it may seem an onerous or boring task, do consider doing it if you are asked. It can offer you rewarding insights as to how the school is run, and what it stands for. It is the governors who should be setting the ethos, and determining the aims of the school, even appointing the head teacher as the senior executive to carry out their wishes. It does not always seem to work like that in practice. Often it seems that the head makes all the decisions and just keeps the governing body informed. This is not so.

Inspectors and advisers will also be interested in how the new style of job is working out, and can report their findings to a wider audience than a governor. It is most likely that you will have experienced being inspected; again openness and confidence will serve you well.

Any *assessor* of your HLTA status should provide quite clear details of the parameters of their visit. For instance, none of them can observe you working in class. Their timetable is strictly controlled by the Teacher Training Agency to ensure that all candidates have similar treatment. Your assessment will be by scrutiny of written documentation and interview. The assessors will also interview the teacher or teachers you work with most closely, and your headteacher or a senior manager responsible for your role. Some of these people within your school may have observed you for appraisal purposes anyway, but will want to observe you in order to be able to report appropriately to the visiting assessor. Do not be worried by such observations. Trainee teachers have many of them and all staff should have appraisal observations at regular intervals. They should be done with your agreement and a clear understanding of purpose, style, timing, place, outcome and appropriate confidentiality. If you have any fears, do voice them to your observer beforehand, so that any discomfort does not mar your performance or affect the outcome for the pupils involved. Sometimes outsiders come to watch your practice (with your permission) because you are so good!

Support partnerships are mainly about the relationships of teachers with *agencies* outside the school and is well worth dipping into if you find a copy (Lacey 2001). She emphasises the importance of learning to work together, for shared learning. Joint INSET, sharing book content or course materials or experiences all help. She suggests using meetings to explore ideas and issues together not just to have a one-way communication about organisational matters or to report progress on a particular pupil. This is particularly relevant when dealing with people outside the school. They will all have something to contribute, if only a different perspective on things within the school. This aspect is particularly important where outside advisers are concerned which may come from a different administrative and professional base such as Health or Social Services. It is only by finding out about each other's role, the ways in which each discipline may have been trained, the expectations of their service and managers, the attitudes and approaches to children and young people as well as colleagues, that you will be able to work together effectively, efficiently and with understanding and enjoyment.

With the publication of *Every Child Matters*, the possibility of working together is increased and the vision for joint working in the same building in the future a real source of hope for joined-up thinking (Clarke *et al.* 2003). However, the adaptations of buildings will need considerable expenditure before such plans become reality. In the meantime the more you can work with, learn about and learn with colleagues from outside the school the better will be the provision of support for the pupils.

You must share with the teachers any information about individual pupils, and ensure records are kept up to date.

Leading a team

Becoming an HLTA could just cause a bit of friction with your TA colleagues, but with sensitivity you should be able to recognise this, understand it, and deal with it. One or two of your colleagues may have wished to be trained instead of you, see you 'getting too big for your boots' or 'above' them. Hopefully the school went through a proper process of selection and appointment for different posts and training opportunities. Look for the positive characteristics in your colleagues, emphasise those, maintain your friendships and support.

Part of your new role may contain a management element. The *Guidance to the Standards* (TTA 2004) clearly states that this management responsibility is not a requirement for HLTA standards, although guiding the work of other adults is [3.3.6]. Working with parent volunteers, visiting speakers and outside professionals would be ways of/opportunities for demonstrating this standard. Nevertheless, many schools will want to use you as a team leader to ease the workload of the SEN coordinator (SENCO) or deputy head or whoever managed the team until you became appointed. One or two schools have even developed senior management teams which consist of senior teachers, the senior TA, midday supervisor, bursar and site manager, recognising the pivotal part such support teams play in the running of the school.

What will be required for assessment purposes in working with other adults, is evidence of joint planning, deploying and briefing the other adults, explaining roles, contexts, objectives, methods and outcomes. This can be in isolated cases as quoted in the guidance like preparing a team of parents before a trip out of school, sports events, or an induction programme for a new TA. Whatever the situation is for you, whether short or longer-term leadership is envisaged, you still need to use similar strategies – those of promoting good relationships. You need sensitivity and tact, good planning with a well thought out programme, give clear advice and consider the teams' personal needs.

Longer-term management, rather than just these one-off situations envisaged by the standards, does require some thought and even training. All the things that have been said about being part of a team apply to being a leader of such a team. All longer-term relationships need time. In school teams, clarity of purpose is required. It would be helpful, at the beginning of taking up any such role that you clarified with the rest of the members:

- the objectives of the team;
- what commitment will be required;
- the purpose and timing of meetings;
- clear roles for members of the group known to all members;
- relationship to other groups and to the whole school team;
- an understanding of any accountability procedures;
- whether working practices of the team will be monitored, mentored or directed from outside;
- what constraints or boundaries the team will be operating within;
- how you all will judge whether the team is successful.

Teams don't just happen by chance. They may have recognised structures set up by themselves or other people, but basically they will be a group of people with feelings, whose contribution needs to be valued. It is a balance between:

- attending to the culture of the group and the structure and organisation;
- enabling continuity yet ensuring appropriate change;

Photograph 4.2   Karalyn Fford, the education officer at Essex Wildlife Trust Abberton reserve with a group of children and adult helpers

- maintenance and innovation;
- openness and trust;
- individual strengths and cooperation;
- cohesiveness and freedom to disagree;
- cooperation and argument.

Be cheerful and optimistic, welcoming to new members and show genuine enthusiasm for what the team achieves. Be considerate. People are not automata. Simple things like cups of tea or buns do help relationships especially at the end of the day. 'Thank yous' are important, a sign of valuing an individual's contribution. Don't gossip about team members or others when in a team meeting. Seek the help of others outside the team if you need it. You are not on your own in a school, and people like to feel they have a contribution to make.

If you are asked to lead a small task group for a particular purpose, such as sorting out the library or the wild life area, remember to have a process of initial activities, then allow development but also recognise there will be decline and withdrawal as the job gets done. Only meet when there is a purpose. If you want the meeting to become informal, get the formalities out of the way efficiently, then break. This allows those that have other demands on their time to decide their priorities. Do what you promise to do; don't promise what you cannot fulfil, delegate whenever you can. People, and children, grow with responsibility. Identify the positive members of the team and try and spread their influence. Teams depend on the variety of contributions of their members. You need thinkers and workers, innovators and those who are more cautious. The whole is greater than the parts and balanced teams of different types of people get results more quickly than teams of uniform people. If you are asked for advice, as the most experienced TA within the team, remember others may have experience in other directions and can helpfully contribute. If you are asked an opinion about members of the team or its work by anyone outside the team remain non-judgemental about other team members and again refer to other team members if it is about their particular role. You are not the sole source of information.

You may get asked to be involved in the interview or induction of new TAs, appraisal or professional development reviews, even mediation. You could be asked to participate in discussion concerning redeployment, even redundancy of fellow TAs. You will certainly begin dealing with personal as well as professional problems. Do take advice and any opportunities for observation or training to help you with such procedures. Professional procedures need to be dealt with correctly or you can cause problems yourself.

An example of good practice

A trip to a nature reserve

The TA told the teacher in charge of the year six class, when they were planning during the summer holidays, that she had enjoyed a recent visit to a reserve with her young family. She suggested that such a visit might fit in with the long-term planning that they were doing for the year ahead. The teacher welcomed this and later made the booking for May the following year directly after SATs week. She talked through the objectives and plan for the day with the reserve education officer. As the TA had experience of the site, the teacher asked her to organise the group of volunteer adults to accompany them on their visit. As the year progressed, a wheelchair bound child joined the class and another TA became attached to the class to be able to attend to the physical needs of the child, which were considerable. Further joint planning now occasionally involved the second TA at the first TA's suggestion. This second TA had contacts among the parent group, so the two TAs drew up a list of whom they might contact. They also asked some of the people who met the children from school. They found they could draw upon a variety of people with different talents. One was the parent of one of the children who spoke Italian at home, one a fireman who did shift work. Another was looked after by grandmother and the last member of their team was a young single mother. All were rather diffident when approached but agreed.

The TA decided that this group should meet before the trip and made arrangements, making a cup of tea for them after school and provided some limited activities for their children while they met. With the agreement of the teacher, she shared the plans for the day, the expectations the teacher and school had regarding behaviour and asked for ideas. She made sure the appropriate checks of the adults were done in the office and that all the other families were aware of who would be helping on the day, particularly the parents of the disabled child. On reaching the reserve the TA had a quick word with the reserve officer and explained the needs of several of the children, particularly the toilet access. The officer was able to provide her with a small walkie-talkie for the support TA in case she got left behind at any point.

The pre-meeting not only ensured the day's visit went smoothly, but proved to be the beginning of a summer's team of help for the class and school. The Italian speaker, who had never visited the school before offered some picture books with photographs of animals and Italian text. Later in the term she came into class and showed them how to make real pizza dough. The fireman, used to lifting, solved all the coach travelling problems for the support TA and arranged a visit of the fire engine to the school fête. The grandmother asked to come in to help with reading in the infant classes, while the young mother proved to relate really well to a couple of disenchanted boys and became friends with their mothers. The TA arranged with a group of year six to set up a small tea party at the end of term for the helpers, to say thank you. The pupils were then able to show off some of the work that had resulted from the visit.

With parents and carers

The example of team working given above is only one possible aspect of your work with parents [1.5]. More and more it is recognised that home influences have a major part to play in the way in which education is perceived by pupils. If education processes are valued by the parents, then their children are likely to value coming to school and working at school tasks. If parents feel supportive of the teaching, they are more likely to support the teachers and support staff. Pupils who truant are often found to be accompanying a parent or close relative, skiving off with their full agreement. You might find that the parent or parents had a poor school experience themselves and have no respect for the adults in the school or what is going on in it. Criticising such people will not help. Try to understand their point of view, even if you do not agree with it, that is what respect means. There is a useful chapter about possible barriers to good relationships with parents in *Parent–Teacher Partnership* (Blamires *et al.* 1997).

As you become an HLTA it is likely that your parent contact will be increased. You may be asked, as in the example above, to organise a small team for a particular purpose, or you may be involved in IEP reviews more or asked to join a teacher on home–school visits. But, you are not a social worker and will not solve all the pupil's problems by yourself. It is another part of team working, where a partnership with the adults in the home will help support the pupil. You may find opportunities to encourage the parents to join in more with school activities, but quiz nights, beetle drives and fêtes are not everybody's cup of tea.

If you have the opportunity to talk with parents about their child's progress, with the understanding of their class teacher, you can help them to understand how and what their child is learning and how they could help at home. It is not a question of them just providing the right books or taking them to museums, although some parents will love doing this, but of helping them understand that an interest in what their children do at school is important to their progress. A place to work or study at home without interruptions and coming into see examples of what they have done, all support the child and make them feel what they do at school is valued. Hopefully, you will not encounter any parents who feel dissatisfied when talking with a TA, even though it is with the support of the teacher and the school, and often in the presence of a teacher, but it can happen even for experienced teachers. There are just a few people who are dissatisfied with everything, or always insist in 'going to the top' whatever they are dealing with – whether buying a car or if their favourite jam is missing from the supermarket shelf.

Consider such meetings as joint problem solving meetings not potential confrontations. If you are a parent, put yourself in their place. If it is a formal meeting you can set the timing, the place, the accommodation, provide refreshments if appropriate and make sure you welcome them. But, if possible set the agenda with the parents so that there is a feeling of partnership. If this is a regular meeting, this will not be a big formal thing. There should be an understanding that there is a mutual interest in the progress and well-being of the pupil or pupils concerned. There should be two-way communication. Listen to what they say, what their focus for action might be. Acknowledge their skills. If there is to be school action following such a meeting be sure you have backing for any suggestions you make and then keep the parents informed of any progress, especially if the action is successful.

Hayes has some useful tips for newly qualified teachers when talking with parents about their children (Hayes 2000). He suggests that there are definite strategies which a teacher can develop to enhance relations when meeting with parents and that they vary depending on whether you are in a formal or informal situation. He sets out the following in diagrammatic form (p. 155):

Always sound enthusiastic when talking about children to their parents:

For informal contacts:

    Sound cheerful and cooperative

    Offer warm eye contact

    Use a natural tone of voice when you speak

Speak positively about children

Take every question seriously

Take a genuine interest in what the parents say

Be wary of making unguarded comments

Avoid being drawn into a lengthy discourse

For formal contacts:

Prepare thoroughly beforehand

Have notes ready about each child

Show that you are pleased to see the parent

Begin by saying something positive

Explain what you are doing to assist the child's learning

Speak honestly but courteously

Don't say any more than necessary

Sound as optimistic as possible

Some reminders when working with parents and volunteers

Not all parents are as literate as you, even in their mother tongue, yet they may be very caring and astute. Written communication may be difficult. There may be linguistic, religious or cultural differences between you and them of which you may be unaware. Be sensitive.

If you are organising parent (or grandparent or other) volunteers to work with pupils, do ensure that they are checked by the office staff in terms of the Criminal Records Bureau according to the policies of the school. These checks can take time to be processed. Do ensure there is some kind of induction training for them before they work in the school, whether or not you are to deliver this.

Induction of parents and volunteers to work with children should cover relevant:

health and safety issues including child protection;

emergency procedures;

confidentiality, punctuality and reliability;

behaviour management strategies available to them in school;

clear parameters of working in terms of areas, designated pupils, appropriate equipment;

> teaching and learning policies – such as use of reading schemes or phonic strategies for those hearing reading or not doing things for pupils in practical sessions;
>
> classroom procedures such as clearing up in time.

This all sounds a bit formal, but starting well can save a lot of heartache later. You may also be able to arrange small demonstrations or workshops to help volunteers understand more about some of the aspects of the work they will be involved in such as reading workshop, or craft work. Sometimes it is a parent who can run something like a pottery or cooking workshop. Do remember though, that these people are volunteers, if they have to go early one day, so be it. Be flexible in preparing any meetings or rotas.

Essential reading

Clarke, C. *et al.* (2003) *Every Child Matters* (Green Paper CYPUECM). London: Department for Education and Skills.

TTA (2004) *Guidance to the Standards – Meeting the Professional Standards for the Award of Higher Level Teaching Assistant Status*. London: Teacher Training Agency.

Any policy concerning customer care or dealing with parents.

Some further reading

Bills, L. (2004) 'Working with parents and other adults' in Brooks, V., Abbott, I. and Bills, L. (eds) *Preparing to Teach in Secondary Schools* pp. 84–95. Maidenhead and New York: Open University Press with McGraw-Hill Education.

Hayes, D. (2000) *The Handbook for Newly Qualified Teachers – Meeting the Standards in Primary and Middle Schools*. London: David Fulton Publishers. Just try pp. 52–61.

Pollard, A. (2002a) *Reflective Teaching – Effective and Evidence-Informed Professional Practice*. London and New York: Continuum. Try pp. 232–3.

Parents

Bastiani, J. (1989) *Working with Parents: A Whole-School Approach*. London: Routledge and NFER-Nelson Publishing Company Limited.

Bastiani, J. (2003) *Materials for Schools: Involving Parents, Raising Achievement*. London: Department for Education and Skills.

Blamires, M. *et al.* (1997) *Parent–Teacher Partnership*. London: David Fulton Publishers.

Useful website

www.dfes.gov.uk/behaviourimprovement/primarypilot/index.cfm – a website to find out more about Sebs.

CHAPTER 5

The context of the whole school

All that you do with pupils and colleagues has to be considered in context. Context makes the difference to how you work and the boundaries of your practice. Figure 5.1 shows how the context in which you work is like being inside a daffodil bulb or an onion.

As an HLTA you must be much more aware of this context than when you just supported an individual child or worked for one teacher. You and your partner teacher will be directing and nurturing the learning of a group of pupils. They all have individual needs whatever you do or whenever you work with them. Classroom operations will be constrained or supported by various levels of interference from outside. The very classroom shape and size, the resources, equipment, other adults and furniture you have access to, will influence the quality of the learning environment which you can provide for the pupils in the class. The school itself will have policies and procedures, and an ethos, culture and vision which will affect these policies and the people who work in the organisation. All of this will take place in a local and national context.

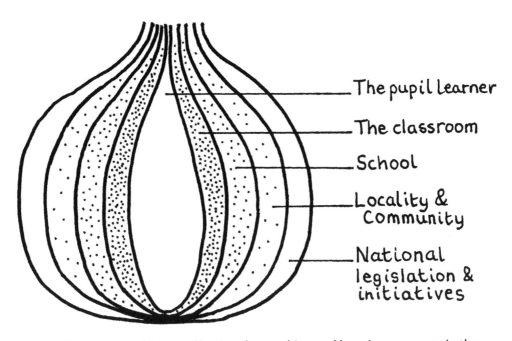

Figure 5.1 The contextual layers affecting the teaching and learning processes in the classroom

School policies and procedures

The best way for you to get a grip on your understanding of school based issues is to work with a teacher mentor and make sure you read some of the school policies if you have not already done so. Most of them will refer to the relevant acts of parliament or circulars from the DfES and explain how these are to be interpreted. While you may feel you would like to go back to the source material, you will find that much of it is written in legal jargon, and hard to read, let alone hard to see where your role fits into the scheme of things.

Policies

The following is a list of school policies and documents which you should look out for and when relevant, take note of. (Having some of these is itself a legal requirement for the school, and these are in italics below. Others may appear in a different form in your school or just be accepted practice rather than spelt out on paper form.) You should get your own copy of some of these policies, or relevant extracts. If your school has a handbook for support staff, or a general handbook, the relevant policies will be specified within it.

Curriculum and teaching and learning strategies, *target setting*, individual subject policies as relevant to you.

Collective worship, sex education, religious education.

Staff appointment, *appraisal, performance management, conduct and grievance.*

Record keeping and confidentiality.

Health and safety, risk assessments and child protection.

Pupil discipline, anti-bullying, behaviour management, conflict resolution.

Equal opportunities including *race equality*, celebrating diversity.

Special educational needs, inclusion, *accessibility*.

Expenditure on resources, *charging*.

Governor and managerial vision, see the *prospectus and annual report to parents.*

Parental involvement, *home–school contract*, working with agencies and advisers.

Staff handbook with arrangements for monitoring, meetings and professional development opportunities.

School development (or improvement) plan and associated plans, *post Ofsted action plan.*

All staff should feel they are able to participate in developing policies, but as an HLTA you should seriously consider this as part of your job, It is not just a question of knowing and complying with them. You are aiming to be in a position of leadership where the other TAs are concerned. You will have views, opportunities to discuss policies with both teachers and other support staff. You will be in a role where you cannot only see what needs doing but should be able to do something about it.

The most likely place is in any review of the SDP. All staff should be consulted, possibly in a questionnaire, or maybe at an INSET day conference. A review of certain policies will then be planned into the year's programme. This will probably mean a small task force will be set up to look into the changes needed and make recommendations which finally end up with the governors for them to approve. This may mean more meetings or consultations, but the result will be an agreed change which all staff can sign up to. If this process is not happening then approach a member of the senior staff or a governor with your concerns.

The needs of the pupils

The centre of my 'bulb' is the pupil learner. The purpose of any school is to advance the learning of the pupils, to get this bulb to flower. So, the learning needs and welfare of those pupils is most important. Often in times of doubt about what to do, you will find it helpful to remind yourself of this. It focuses the mind on what really matters.

Many, if not most of you, will have come into the job of being a teaching assistant through supporting individual children with SEN. You are therefore probably familiar with the code of practice for SEN, individual education plans (IEPs) and the school's policy in this area. If you are not familiar, you must make a special point of doing so, as standard 2.8 particularly refers to this. In an inclusive school, it is recommended that class teachers draw up IEPs, not the SENCO, so that the support for pupils with SEN can be part of the regular work of the class. The SENCO will give advice, keep records, monitor the pupil's development and IEP implementation, undertake reviews and ensure the various parts of the process take part smoothly. Where this happens, and you are involved with the teacher's planning, you also will be clear about intentions. You will be probably very famil- iar with how the IEPs are drawn up, operate, and are reviewed. You may well participate in the review system, organised by the SENCO.

In other schools, the IEPs are drawn up by the SENCO and support for the pupil may be by their withdrawal from class for special attention. Where inclusion rather than inte- gration is high on the aspirations of the school managers, withdrawal is limited. However, for some areas of support, especially in areas like physiotherapy, withdrawal is not only unavoidable but advisable. Timing of this can be a matter for concern, in order that the pupil does not miss something else by being out of the room at the time of it happening. Sometimes, the pupil may need to catch up away from the class. Occasionally, withdrawal of a disturbed pupil is for the benefit of the rest of the class.

You should know what the role of an educational psychologist is in your school, and any other adviser or therapist who visits relevant to the pupils you support. In some schools, it is the TA who does the liaising and reports back to the teacher, to save the teacher leaving the class.

Code of practice

You should get a copy of the code of practice (DfES 2001) for yourself.

You won't remember all the details and do not have to, but you will find it fairly readable.

The foreword gives the context of the code. Even if you work as a general assistant in mainstream schools, you should still have an understanding of the process and be able to demonstrate how you can support pupils with SEN in class.

Read the earlier chapters on principles and policies, working in partnership with parents and pupil participation.

Choose to read Chapters 4, 5 or 6 depending on which phase you work in.

Skim the pages on statutory assessment, statement and annual reviews just to get a feel for the recommendations.

(The actual SEN legislation forms the latter part of the book. You will quickly see what I meant by legal jargon if you try to read these pages!)

The emphasis on SEN has rightly drawn attention and funding to a group of pupils who were underachieving because of lack of support. Many of you will also have worked with groups during the literacy or numeracy strategy who have been identified as needing extra support to reach the target levels for their ages, but who have not been identified as having SEN or are on any register. For further guidance on SEN provision do talk with your SENCO even if you are not line managed by them. Part of their job is to be a specialist in the area and they will point you to courses, resources, books and websites which will support you in whatever you wish to do. David Fulton Publishers have a long list of very accessible books on specific needs if any of the pupils you work with have these.

Removing Barriers to Achievement (DfES 2004a) reinforces many ideas already in practice, wanting the good practice seen to be in all schools. It covers early intervention, removing barriers in mainstream and special schools, raising expectations and improving partnerships with agencies and parents. You can keep up to date on the developments in the government's ideas for those with SEN through the teachernet website.

Another group you should consider is very bright pupils. These can sometimes be ignored in planning, as a teacher may consider them well able to get on on their own. There is now much more advice for the gifted and talented (or G&Ts as they are sometimes referred to), some authorities even having G&T advisers. The Qualifications and Curriculum Authority (QCA) document reference in the Annex A list is helpful here, as is the QCA website. There is additional material available to support G&T pupils to be found on the curriculum and teachernet websites. It is unlikely the SENCO will deal with this area as SEN is usually associated with those who have problems or impairments rather than the other end of the spectrum. Some schools will have an identified teacher who has sources of information and resources in the same way as the SENCO for those with SEN. Ask around.

While it is tempting to identify those pupils who do have needs in addition to the average ones, in reality all pupils have differing needs, and these will also vary with circumstances. The government's ideas on the 'personalisation' of learning is really about making sure that all pupils' needs are considered, not about teaching each child a different curriculum or teaching all pupils individually.

It is also important, to remember that emotional and social needs affect how a child – or an adult – learns. These are not legislated for in the same way as the SEN or G&T needs are specified, but may well be in your school policies. There will be more about this aspect in the accompanying book.

Health, safety and security

Whatever you do in school for and with the pupils or adults must be done with regard to health and safety matters. There is legislation which covers all employees in whatever kind of employment they find themselves, and there is legislation and guidance covering the particular environment of a school. Make sure you have seen your school's documents dealing with health and safety or know where they are. Hopefully, your induction to the school included all aspects of this from dealing with emergencies to long-term sickness arrangements.

Check the following:

If you are working in a laboratory or design and technology area:

> Copies of guidance from the Association for Science Education:
>> for primary schools: *Be Safe* (ASE 2001) and
>> for secondary schools: *Safeguards in School Laboratories* (ASE 1996)
>
> from the Design and Technology Association:
>> *Primary Design and Technology: A Guide for Teaching Assistants* (DATA 1996)

Emergency and security procedures, dealing with fire, bomb alerts, intruders, use of alarms, and so on.

General Safety Precautions: Avoiding Hazards and Staying Healthy (LSC 2003)

Educational Visits and Adventures (DfEE 1998a) (DfES 2002a)

Supporting Children with Medical Needs (DfEE 1996)

Guidance on First Aid for Schools (DfEE 1998b)

Drugs or Substance Misuse (DfES 2004c)

Physical contact and intervention:

Tackling Bullying – Don't Suffer in Silence (DfEE 2000)

The Use of Force to Control or Restrain Pupils (DfEE 1998c)

Dealing with Harassment or Racist Incidents

One of the best ways to understand such procedures is to imagine as many awful situations as you can and think through what you would do. If you can do this with colleagues it makes it more interesting and helpful. Try taking it in turns to ask the awkward question and discuss what you would do.

What do you do if:

a child trips and cuts themselves and you are the only one present?

you are asked to take a group to the local shop?

a pupil calls another pupil a 'black bastard'?

you come across a fight between two boys taller and stronger than you?

you find a strange adult with no identification label carrying a leather tool bag?

you are with a pupil with SEN in a school laboratory and another pupil spills some acid?

you are with a group in the environmental area at the far side of the playing field and one has an epileptic fit?

you are asked to take the new paper stock to the stock cupboard?

you are asked to put up a high display in the hall?

you are being bullied yourself by your line manager to take a class for a whole afternoon a week when you know the class teacher will not let you have access to her plans or talk about what she would do?

you find pupils smoking in the playground after school has finished?
a parent threatens you physically?

Every child matters

One of the latest sets of documents relevant to working with pupils is not in the HLTA Annex A list. After the Victoria Climbié inquiry, following the death of the little girl in 2000 in the care of her aunt, the working of the 1989 Children Act was reviewed and certain recommendations were put forward. The definition of 'children' is anyone under the age of 18. The green paper *Every Child Matters* (Clarke *et al.* 2003), mentioned in the last chapter, was published in 2003. There was a wide consultation including with young people themselves. This was followed by *Every Child Matters – The Next Steps* (DfES 2004d). During autumn 2004 a children's bill went through parliament to put into law some of the recommendations. These were wide ranging and affecting all the authorities who have dealings with care: Education, Social Services, Health and the Police; and requiring them to work closer together. This is not just to be at county hall level but at school level, which is why this green paper was mentioned in the chapter on relationships. School staff will be having ever closer relationships with workers from these agencies as the recommendations are put into practice.

The aims in the green paper were to achieve the outcomes that matter most to children and young people:

Being healthy: enjoying good mental and physical health and living a healthy lifestyle.

Staying safe: being protected from harm and neglect.

Enjoying and achieving: getting the most out of life and developing the skills of adulthood.

Making a positive contribution: being involved with the community and society and not engaging in anti-social or offending behaviour.

Economic well-being: not being prevented by economic disadvantage from achieving their full potential in life.

The House of Lords added *leisure* and *emotional well being* but these were not in the final bill.

The proposals included *full service extended schools* which open beyond school hours to provide breakfast and after school clubs and childcare, and have health and social care support services on site. Clearly there are a lot of planning, logistical and personnel problems to be tackled before this could become a reality. Professionals will be encouraged to work in multi-disciplinary teams based in and around schools. Children's centres, are to be developed from Sure Start centres, to provide rapid responses to concerns and a more 'joined-up' approach than is currently possible.

Child protection procedures

Recently, the guidance document *Safeguarding Children in Education* (DfES 2004e) was published. This indicates that the Circular 10/95, *Protecting Children from Abuse – The Role of the Education Service*, mentioned in Annex A, is now superseded. Your headteacher will be taking note of this new guidance as it is written for those in schools, FE colleges and LEAs, responsible for management of such issues. It gives guidance on safeguarding and promoting the welfare of children as laid down in the 2002 Education Act, which came into force in June 2004. It is not about what you as an individual should do if you are worried about a pupil. The new guidance suggests training in child protection matters for all staff should be on induction and at three yearly intervals. If this is not so in your school, do ask about it. The guidance also gives help about protecting staff from false allegations and a useful list of other relevant guidance. Some of this other guidance is also in your Annex A list.

There is helpful material in the updated version of the DfES induction training for TAs, the role and context module. The child protection element has been enhanced to reflect the new developments. The definition of child abuse given there covers any action whereby 'a child is hurt or harmed by another person in a way that causes significant harm to that child and which may well have an effect on the child's development or well being' (DfES 2004f). Do ensure you understand the various types of abuse and what to do if you suspect there is a problem. It is the role of the social services and the police to investigate, not schools.

If you are worried about potential child abuse:

Get the document *What to Do if You're Worried that a Child is Being Abused* (DH *et al.* 2003).

The initial useful pages define need, harm, abuse and neglect.

> Abuse can be physical or emotional or sexual, or due to neglect.

Page 7 gives guidance for all practitioners.

> Listen carefully to what the child has to say; do not question or put words in their mouth.

> Do not promise confidentiality about any disclosure.

> Keep notes of what has been heard, seen or told and when.

> Discuss the matter with the named person in your school – the senior designated teacher (SDT).

> Do not discuss the matter with the child's parents unless it is part of an agreed strategy.

> Do not do anything which may jeopardise any later investigation, like asking leading questions or attempting to investigate matters for yourself.

> Do not make any referral yourself. This is the role of the named person in your school.

> Ensure you get proper training in the matters.

Consistency and confidentiality

If you operate the same policies regarding health, safety and security matters, behaviour management strategies and carry out the teachers' instructions in the way that the school has laid down, there will be the minimum of confusion for the pupils. The boundaries, and consequences for breaking them, will be the same whoever is the adult. Consistency of practice enables pupils to feel secure and provides a learning environment which facilitates curriculum progression. Consistency, communication, and a positive climate with the need for whole school policies, and plans, were three of the key factors identified as contributing to what makes effective schools (Mortimore *et al.* 1988; Sammons and Mortimore 1995).

Communication within an organisation is also important. Instructions, boundaries of responsibility, levels of action do need to be spelt out explicitly. TAs as well as teachers need to know of organisational or policy changes that are proposed. In large schools this is bound to mean more paper to read, and paying attention in meetings. HLTAs will have to be included in meetings, and should be in a position to communicate with the rest of the TA team [3.3.6].

The loyalty that develops in any school, for staff to each other and to the leadership however weak, including those with low expectations is striking. The need for confidentiality and professionalism among those who work in school can create a difficulty that you should think about from time to time. Recently there has been a lot in the press about whistleblowing in organisations in general, and the possibility of harassment and bullying from senior staff, including schools. What should you do if you observe something or are told something that should be dealt with to make life more bearable for some member of staff or a group of pupils? Parents have their complaints procedure. As a team leader, you may be in the position to have to investigate a problem for a colleague. You could even be a victim yourself. It is recommended that schools have a policy which helps staff deal with such problems as harassment [3.3.7], but this still does not help your feelings, your discomfort, the difficulty of continuing to work in an organisation where you may have been responsible for upsetting the *status quo*.

Consider some more what-ifs

What are you to do if you find a member of your TA team is being asked to leave by a senior manager because she has been late and absent on too many occasions. You know that she has a frail elderly mother who is very demanding, and is a single parent with two school age children. Where do your loyalties lie?

What do you do if you know the headteacher is having an affair with a member of staff?

What do you do if you see a teacher shake a very aggressive child?

What do you do if you are of a non-white racial origin, and some parents have asked their children not to ask you for help?

What do you do if your friend's child is being 'picked on' by a teacher?

From whom do you seek help?

The whole school

In our country, it is interesting to see that individual schools do not 'jump on band wagons'. They have their own values and principles which are often openly debated:

> . . . the values of the schools which seem to us to be successful is that their values are not of the market place: they are not preoccupied with 'getting one over' on competitor schools, but are

simply determined not to be undermined by them . . . [The leaders] show genuine concern for the work of all the staff, not just some. There seems to be real commitment to celebrating the achievement of all pupils rather than a few. [They have] the ability to convince those outside school of the confident pride in all that the school community achieves together with its restless determination and expectation to achieve more rather than sit back on its laurels'. (Brighouse and Woods 1999: 51)

The authors go on to say, that although the values may be written down in statements of aims, 'It is the way they are talked about in day-to day activities that values are established'. Do join in such debates. It is the sharing of these values, having a shared vision that gives all staff a common purpose, 'nourishes a sense of commitment' and guides practice (Senge *et al.* 2000: 8).

A school can have all the policies it likes, obey all the directives from the government but it will not be a successful school in the full sense of the word if the relationships within the school are not right. The climate of the school depends first on the ethos set by the leadership at all levels. But it shows in the relationships of all those working in the school have to each other. The learning environment which the pupils encounter will depend on the way in which the adults who organise it, work together and with the available resources.

Ethos and climate

It is clear from the work on values education and inclusion that the areas of ethos and climate, although difficult to define, are crucial to the way in which a school operates. They influence the way people and pupils behave to each other, and provides the foundation for budgetary, staffing, equipment, and systems decisions. It was clear from the research I did into the ways in which TAs operate, that the ethos and culture of the school influenced the outcomes for their work with children. A few schools that I have visited with a negative culture, have been characterised by negative attitudes to educational change. The staff were friendly, but reluctant to talk about educational matters. Their morale was low, and this would be seen in the way they spoke about pupils, often critically. The TAs tended to be less active in the classroom, and suspicious of suggestions for improvement. Sadly, these schools were also characterised by poor or weak leadership from the head, often through no fault of his or her own. The head sometimes was unwell or had been away ill. Sometimes they were long serving and rather bored or disillusioned, unfortunately sometimes just incompetent. Discipline tended to be negative – 'Don't do that', rather than constructive or positive. Praise and celebration were rarer. Thankfully, such schools are rare.

Two schools, which I studied closely, had a very supportive culture. All staff were valued including the TAs, and they knew that they were. This was not a result of high salaries, but acceptance as part of a whole school team. They were consulted and they offered ideas. Different ways of training, evaluating, planning, even meeting together were tried out. New formats of documents could come from the TAs to the teaching staff as well as the other way. There was laughter in the staffroom, educational books, magazines, and videos were shared. Pupils' needs were discussed positively and their achievements, however small were celebrated. Staff achievements were celebrated.

Developing ethos

Schools Speak for Themselves gives 12 indicators of ethos which were developed by the Scottish Office Education Department. Try out these indicators for yourself. The suggestion is that members of the school community can rate them from 1 to 4, 1 being excellent, and then group together to share their results and reach a compromise to obtain a final score.

- Pupil morale
- Teacher morale
- Teachers' job satisfaction
- The physical environment
- The learning context
- Pupil–teacher relationships
- Discipline
- Equality and justice
- Extra-curricular activities
- School leadership
- Information to parents
- Parent teacher consultation. (MacBeath *et al.* 1996: 97)

If this nebulous thing called ethos is positive and working, the school climate, what you actually feel when you go into the school is also positive. Schools quite clearly have a feel to them. If you go in as a visitor, and I have visited hundreds of schools now, you can feel welcome whether or not there is a security system. You can see the care taken in surroundings. You can see the smile on the receptionist's face. You can hear laughter and children's chat. You can sense the tone of the teacher's voice even if the pupil is being reprimanded. You may well have felt this if you have visited schools when having to decide where you want your child to go to school.

'School climate is the heart and soul of a school. It is about the essence of a school that leads a child, an administrator, a staff member to love the school and look forward to being there each day. School climate is about that quality of a school that helps each individual feel personal worth, dignity and importance, while simultaneously helping to create a sense of belonging to something beyond ourselves' (Freiberg and Stein 1999: 11).

The five key features of school climate could be:

- 'The schools is a happy place to be.
- There are places for pupils to go and constructive things to do outside class time.
- Pupils and staff behave in a relaxed and orderly way.

- Pupils, staff and parents feel that their contribution to the school is valued.

- The school is welcoming to visitors and newcomers'. (MacBeath *et al.* 1996: 34)

Another word used in this context is culture – 'the ultimate ceiling on our ability to transform our school and raise standards ... a reservoir of energy and wisdom to sustain motivation and co-operation, shape relationships and aspirations and guide effective choices at every level of the school'. (Hobby 2004: 6) Following some investigations of cultures and values in successful schools, Hobby and his colleagues come up with some interesting theories of why such schools are succeeding.

Try the following out on your colleagues and discuss their responses:

- The role of a school is to provide opportunities for all.

- Teaching can be improved through sharing best practice and working together.

- High expectations and ambitions are both appropriate and can produce real gains.

- Achievement in test results is an 'output' of the education system. The ability to learn is an 'input'. The two are connected and success in the outputs follows on an investment in the inputs. The two must be considered together.

- The function of a school extends beyond academic and exam success to preparing the foundations for a student's broader life.

- Attention should be divided equally, not on the basis of ability to succeed.

- Students' potential may often surprise us.

- Teaching quality will rise when teachers are held accountable for their performance and standards are 'owned' by the school not the individual.

- The comfort of staff is secondary to the needs of students. Schools are service-based organisations.

- Ambition is not the same as elitism.

- We cannot be sure what environment (careers, social and economic trends) we are preparing our students for.

- Well intentioned failures are not acceptable over the long term. (Hobby 2004: 48)

The whole of Balshaw's book on *Help in the Classroom* (Balshaw 1999) where she outlines an INSET package for developing assistants for support in the classroom, is based on the premise that such training only works where the climate is right. In fact, she includes a health warning, pointing out that raising some of the issues which she tackles, where the climate is not right, can be dangerous.

Case study evidence

Teachers, senior management and TAs referred to the 'St So-and-so's way' or of 'one big family' when describing the behaviour of the adults. The senior management looked forwards as well as recognising the changes taking place at the time. TAs and teachers talked of future training, of how to manage the fluctuating budget with its various pockets to the best advantage of the people in the team as well as the children, how they would like a male TA to serve as a role model, particularly for some of the more disturbed boys with dysfunctional family backgrounds. All the staff treated each other and the pupils with politeness and expected to be treated in the same way by the pupils: doors were held open for someone, adult or child carrying a load or hurrying; school work, notices and messages were expected to be legible; drawers or shelves were to be left tidy whoever they belonged to. Pupils or staff with emotional problems were treated with understanding. Understanding of staff's personal background featured high in conversations and humour infiltrated many conversations. This meant that the TAs could challenge and provide companionship and humour for those carrying greater responsibility. They were sources of local understanding and contacts, and in this school provided a parental point of view to a teaching staff team with few teachers who were parents. 'The equation has become unbalanced . . . but we'll work it out'. TAs were part of any social event organised by or for the teaching staff (Watkinson 2003c: 58).

In another school, with a relatively new head, the TAs described the changes they had undergone when the head decided to change their job descriptions from supporting pupils with SEN to one supporting literacy and numeracy. They were to be allocated to particular teachers and mainly were going to come in for mornings only. All were requested to be present in school on a Wednesday for a meeting with the head, who was also the SENCO. These changes had come about after consultation with all the staff as to how the new strategies could best be implemented for the good of all the pupils. Once the new system started, the TAs suggested new forms to complete about their work so that there would be consistency between classes. They were helping write their own TA policy. TAs were meeting teachers in the school holidays to plan jointly.

School relationships

There are some useful questions to discuss with your mentor about school relationships. This could open up some sensitive areas, and many of which you may be unable to influence, but the more all staff consider these, the more likely any areas of concern can be improved. School relationships are not just about getting on well with people or pupils, everyday social intercourse. 'For the *intelligent school* good relationships and exchange of experience do not stop at the classroom door but are positively encouraged across the school and, indeed, are essential to building the school as a healthy, sustainable community. While students are developing the skills of learning to learn, they are doing so with each other and their teachers in a range of settings, and their teachers are learning about learning' (MacGilchrist *et al.* 2004: 133).

Questions about school relationships

Are all staff consulted and involved in decision making in school?

Are support staff involved in policy formation?

Are pupils asked their opinions? Can their views be used?

Are pupils helpful or unsupportive of each other?

Are some groups of pupils regularly found isolated by other pupils or appear regularly outside the head's room or frequently get labelled as lazy, stupid or naughty?

Are differences of opinion, conflicts, and so on discussed openly in classrooms? The staffroom?

Do all staff feel valued members of the school?

How welcome do parents feel in the school?

How welcome do governors feel in the school?

Does the school reach out to those sections of the community/parents which are less involved in the school?

What opportunities are there for parents and the school to share their hopes and expectations?

How accessible is the head teacher to the pupils, the staff and the parents?

How do we show that the opinions and help and support of parents and/or governors are valued?

What opportunities are there for the pupils to link with the community?

Is the school an Investor in People? Do you know what that means for the school?

Learning environment

While much of the school climate is about people's attitudes to each other and pupils, some of it is about care of the environment, the provision of a place where people want to spend time, and to spend that time in learning. Provision of interesting displays, accessible, clean and colourful book collections, photographs of events or people who serve the school, all point to a place where people care. The state of the toilets, both for staff and pupils, has a lot to say about whether the school cares about people who use them, and whether the people using them care about how they use them. Organisation of school equipment for easy access, tidy and ready for use, gives the message of a place where learning is encouraged.

School grounds maintenance, style of lunchtime service, notice boards and communication formats all give messages of care, interest, fitness for purpose, or not.

Try out the following:

What does a visitor see in your school?

Care of the environment:

Was it easy to find the car park and reception?

Is the entry foyer welcoming?

Are the plants watered?

Are notices up to date?

Is there somewhere for a visitor to sit when waiting?

Would you like to sit there if it was the doctors' or a hotel reception area?

Is available documentation reader friendly?

Is there display showing valuing of pupils' work?

Are rooms labelled, and fire exits clear?

The way people behave:

What is the attitude of the receptionist to telephone calls?

Do receptionists make eye contact with visitors even if they are busy on the telephone?

Do receptionists make sure whether visitors need a drink or the lavatory?

How do receptionists hand over to a member of staff?

Is the visitors' book/fire register properly maintained?

Who shows visitors round the school?

How do adults speak to each other in the corridor?

How do pupils talk to visitors?

Who smiles?

What are the noise levels? (Watkinson 2003c: 57)

The photographs overleaf show how one urban school involved parents and pupils in improving the visual appearance of their site and provided a learning area for the pupils as well.

Whole school development

Developing a whole school is not a top-down thing, even though it depends on good leadership for things to be carried through. It is about involving people and pupils,

An example of good practice

A year three class was observed in a large urban school with a very mixed catchment area where the school council had been functioning for a couple of terms. Already the children had elected a chairperson, school council representatives and a minute taker and had learnt the basic rules of such debate. The teacher stood to one side at the front and observed proceedings. The class knew they had about half an hour before break to discuss the feedback from the school council and propose any new ideas which their representatives could put forward at the next full meeting. The chairperson, a small girl, who had been rather insignificant in the general class work, chaired the meeting better than many adults observed in similar circumstances. She noted who wanted to speak and took them in order and limited their time speaking. She could extract the essence of the debate to sum up, and managed to conclude proceedings about the right time. Members of the class recognised that given their turn, they could contribute and their views were considered by their peers. This meant they did not shout out or interrupt. The teacher did not intervene except to enable the activity to begin and end appropriately. It was impressive.

and enabling those not at the top to have a voice – including the pupils. Some useful work is done in schools which have instituted a school council, where the teachers have trained the class to carry out those skills mentioned in group work but on a larger scale – listening, sharing, joint problem solving, decision making, delegating jobs and recording activities.

In *The Intelligent School* (MacGilchrist *et al.* 2004) the authors describe another intelligence which they call 'collegial intelligence' which has four aspects: commitment to a shared purpose; knowledge creation; multilevel learning and trust and curiosity. They explain that just coming together, supporting each and working together is not enough to ensure improvement. It is about ownership of purpose, interdependence and asking questions. They also describe reflective intelligence, where not only do individuals reflect on their practice but the whole institution does.

Senge, an American with an industrial background working in the field of organisational dynamics has much to offer in consideration of how schools work. His ideas have been helpful, particularly with the concept of the learning organisation. Basically, his thesis can be reduced to the idea that the whole is greater than the sum of the parts, but that all the parts matter. He suggests teams working together are the fundamental units of organisations. Any organisation needs *systems*, but it also needs all the members to have what he calls *personal mastery* of their job. There need to be *mental models* of what is going on, a *shared vision* of what is possible, but most importantly *team learning*, his *Fifth Discipline* (Senge 1990).

Where the school is secure in its aims, and has a positive ethos and collaborative culture, where relationships are good and team members can challenge each other with respect, the systems and procedures will provide the machinery to carry out the aims. Adults can enjoy their time in the school and provide enhanced opportunities for learning. (Watkinson 2003c: 39)

Photograph 5.1 The working party

Photograph 5.2 The result

This is me
Digging up the
ground.

Photograph 5.3 Pupil work following the pupil involvement

The illustrations come from the scrapbook compiled to record
the development at Hinguar Community Primary School,
Southend-on-Sea.

Stoll and Fink believe that change is necessary for organisations to improve, as they will either improve or decline. They also develop the concept of a school as a learning organisation, suggesting that as such they have certain qualities:

- Professional teachers treated as such.
- High quality staff development.
- Teacher leadership.
- Collaboration respecting individuality.
- Induction processes.
- Functioning well within a wider community.
- Working to change things that matter.
- Processes and procedures that staff, pupils and parents trust. (Stoll and Fink 1995)

Questions you can ask yourself

Do you think you are in an improving school? How can you tell?

Does anything in your school need changing? Such as?

How powerless are you really in the school hierarchy to question or change anything?

Will your change of role make any difference?

Do you get on with everybody?

Do you need to change any of your ways or attitudes?

Are the talents of any of your colleagues being ignored?

What could you do about it?

Here are some interesting guidelines for action if you consider change is needed given in *What's Worth Fighting For in Your School*. They are intended for teachers but are surely relevant to HLTAs:

1 Locate, listen to and articulate your inner voice.
2 Practise reflection in action, on action and about action.
3 Develop a risk-taking mentality.
4 Trust processes as well as people.
5 Appreciate the total person in working with others.
6 Commit to working with colleagues.
7 Seek variety and avoid balkanisation.

8 Redefine you role to extend beyond the classroom.

9 Balance work and life.

10 Push and support heads and other administrators to develop interactive professionalism.

11 Commit to continuous improvement and perpetual learning.

12 Monitor and strengthen the connection between your development and the students' development. (Fullan and Hargreaves 1992: 86)

Essential reading

DfES (2001) *Special Educational Needs Code of Practice*. London: Department for Education and Skills.

DH, HO, DfES, DCMS, ODPM, and LC (2003) *What to Do if You're Worried that a Child is Being Abused* (31553). London: Department of Health, Home Office, Department of Education and Skills, Department for Culture, Media and Sport, Office of the Deputy Prime Minister and the Lord Chancellor.

LSC (2003) *Be Safe*. London: Learning and Skills Council.

The summary of DfES, Clarke, C., Boateng, P. and Hodge, M. (2003) *Every Child Matters* (Green Paper CYPUECM). London: Department for Education and Skills.

Some further reading

Ideology and issues

DfES (2004b) *Working Together – Giving Young People a Say* (DfES/0134/2004). London: Department for Education and Skills.

Leadbeater, C. (2004) *Learning About Personalisation: How Can We Put the Learner at the Heart of the Education System?* London: Department for Education and Skills in partnership with DEMOS and the National College for School Leadership.

Matheson, D. (2004) 'What is education?', in Matheson D., (ed.) *An Introduction to a Study of Education,* 2nd edn. London: David Fulton Publishers, pp. 1–16.

Worth dipping into if you find a copy

Hobby, R. (2004) *A Culture for Learning*. London: The Hay Group Management Ltd.

Mortimore, P. *et al.* (1988) *School Matters*. Wells: Open Books Publishing.

Senge, P. M. *et al.* (2000) *Schools that Learn*. London and Yarmouth, USA: Nicholas Brealey Publishing.

Possibly useful

If your school has not used the LEA induction courses – contain updated child protection materials.

DfES (2004f) *Role and Context Module: Induction Training for Teaching Assistants in Primary Schools*. London: Department for Education and Skills.

DfES (2004g) *Role and Context Module: Induction Training for Teaching Assistants in Secondary Schools*. London: Department for Education and Skills.

DfES (2004h) *Teaching Assistant File: Induction Training for Teaching Assistants in Primary Schools*. London: Department for Education and Skills.

DfES (2004i) *Teaching Assistant File: Induction Training for Teaching Assistants in Secondary Schools*. London: Department for Education and Skills.

CHAPTER 6

The local and national context

Remember the analogy of the bulb in Chapter 5? It can be taken further. Picture the bulb before it is planted and then after it is planted. The soil, weather and feeding the bulb enable it to grow, to put down roots of tradition and produce a shoot and eventually a flower – the growth of learning. The external environment affects the development of the whole bulb, all those layers of context. These influences could be things like the training and professional development of anyone involved at any level. The interest of the general public and parents in particular in educational matters also affects the growth. Research into educational processes, evaluations of projects and initiatives should possibly have more influence than they do. Funding will of course affect provision, the development of all of the layers.

The training of HLTAs is a case in point. The funding of this project is part of a much wider workforce remodelling initiative, of which more later in this chapter. This initiative has government funding, a national group working on materials, LEA and school based teams, affecting all staff in school with the expressed aim of raising standards of achievement in pupils. You may be just one among many considering your role in the scheme. While the initiative will release talent in people such as you, and release teachers to have a better work-life balance, it is being done so that children and young people will have the best possible chance of learning.

Schools, and the education they provide, exist in a legal framework as do so many aspects of our lives. Even parents are not free to do just what they like with their own children. There is a legal obligation on them to have their children educated – either at school or under a registered and inspected system of education at home. State schools operate under more regulations than independent schools. Independent schools may not have to follow the NC, although some do. They may not have qualified teachers in front of classes, although most do. Even these schools have to operate within a system of inspection and certain acts of parliament such as the Race Relations Act, employment law and Health and Safety at Work legislation.

Annex A in the guidance to the standards for HLTA status gives a list of some of the regulatory documents which affect support staff. Many of them affect all staff. You do not have to get copies of all these, read them and understand them to fulfil the criteria for standard 2.7. Many heads and qualified teachers would be hard put to it to find these documents let alone know and understand the detail of their contents. Note the statement in the guidance: 'This standard does not require support staff to have detailed knowledge of all these, but they should be aware that such a range of documents exist and that it covers key issues such as health and safety, special educational needs, child protection

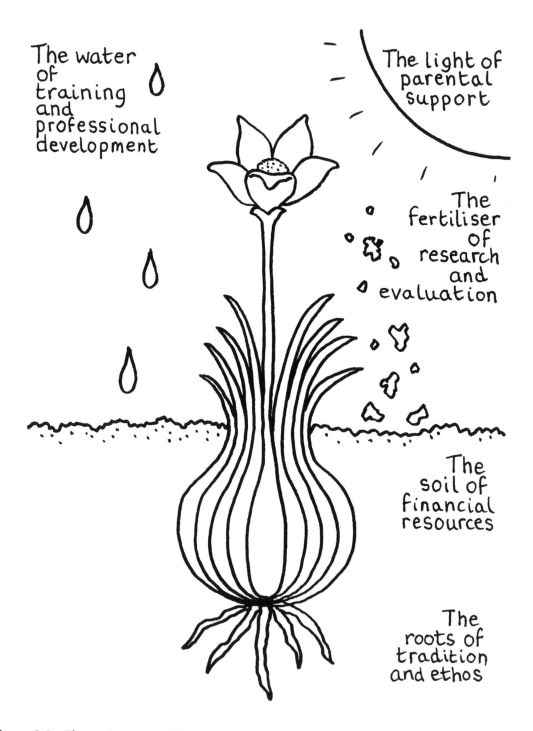

The water of training and professional development

The light of parental support

The fertiliser of research and evaluation

The soil of financial resources

The roots of tradition and ethos

Figure 6.1 The environment of learning growth

and employment. They need to be aware that they have rights and responsibilities as employees as well as in their role as support staff' (TTA 2004: 17).

Community and locality influences

One of the things that makes every school different is the locality or community in which it is situated. The difference between a rural school and an urban one can be very significant. The pupils in a rural area are more likely to come to school by bus. This means they will have a longer day than their urban counterparts. They may become tired more quickly or have difficulty in accessing libraries or similar for homework. However, they may have a greater understanding of environmental matters. Their playgrounds are more likely to have a grass area and their homes more likely to have gardens. Employment background will affect the pupils. In areas of high unemployment, aspects of poverty and deprivation will be seen, along with attitudes towards working and the usefulness or otherwise of schools. Schools serving a big garrison have to cope with rapid and frequent turnover of large groups of children as troops and their families are moved from one area to another. Prosperous areas will have increased funding due to well-patronised fundraising activities and motivated parents. You must respect the background of all pupils and try to understand the things that may prevent their learning or sense of well being or self-esteem [1.1].

A salutary experience

Reported by a headteacher – food for thought

The school was in the middle of a 1920s estate in a deprived area of a large town in South Eastern England. The town was prosperous, employment levels high although largely in service industries not manufacturing. The level of unemployment, domestic violence, drug abuse, petty and more serious crime and even child abuse in this particular area was high. The estate was geographically limited and identifiable. Few pupils came to the school from out of the area. The head could be involved in anything up to half a dozen case conferences a term and had been threatened with physical violence from parents on occasions. However, there was a full complement of dedicated staff. The head, with the staff had tackled the behaviour management issues. There was little if any truancy. Teacher morale was high and curriculum issues well discussed. The learning environment was being addressed and improvements to the building slowly underway, although local fundraising was low. However, assessment results showed very low scores, only 20 to 30 per cent reaching their target levels.

Taking a year five class one morning, the head gave them a writing exercise of imagining what they would be doing in ten years' time – by which time they would mainly be about 20 years old. The highest aspiration was that of one girl who hoped to be a veterinary nurse. About half the class reckoned they would be unemployed and living on benefits at home. Some thought they might have a job in a local shop such as a tile centre, and only a few thought they might have jobs further afield or undertake any training after leaving school. All assumed they would have left school at 16. Many of the girls assumed they would be mothers; marriage was mentioned by many. None mentioned higher education or any 'white collar' job.

The question posed was how can a school staff act to raise self-esteem in such surroundings, let alone reach curriculum targets, without denigrating the backgrounds of many of the families sending their children to the school.

It can and has been done!

Cultural background influences school life and a diversity can bring a richness to school life that a more homogenous background lacks. Racism is still prevalent in some areas where there are homogenous ethnic communities and newcomers in any great number are seen as a threat. It is not just a problem for deprived areas. It can happen in prosperous areas, where houses sell to second home purchasers, or where recently arrived immigrants join their already established families and friends. It is hard for school staff to celebrate diversity or increase respect for all cultures in such places. Support is needed for communication, often where different languages are spoken, but also in interpreting the ways in which different people behave, dress, enjoy leisure time or worship. It is not just about respect but also about being positive about what the pupils can bring from home, the added dimensions that diversity can bring.

You must be aware of any racial prejudice that pupils might voice, and even possibly in the staffroom. All schools should have an anti-racism policy, do ensure you read a copy.

Some good practice

Picture a London overspill town in the late 1990s, where housing for those wishing to leave the East End of London greatly expanded a small country town about 50 miles from London in the early 1960s. Employment was high. Factory building had accompanied the housing developments and the local train service was good to neighbouring towns or London. Leisure centres, schools, libraries and similar facilities had been built and were well used. The increase in population meant the town also supported a secondary school, and flourishing shops, selling the merchandise required by the community. Signs of the original town were few and were located in a small area round the old church. Several primary schools built to serve the area had a totally white population. Despite the fact that the new population came from a limited part of London, the upheaval of moving large groups of people, breaking families away from their wider roots and settling in a new environment had brought with it considerable family stress. Behaviour management in the schools was not easy. Literacy and numeracy were not high and were priorities long before the strategies were introduced.

Two TAs, working both in the nursery and the reception class in one school were supported by the school in undertaking an early years NVQ. In doing this, they found the process put considerable emphasis on celebrating cultural diversity and anti-discrimination. They struggled to see how this could take place in their school. Parents had even complained when reading books with pictures of Black and Asian children in them were taken home. With the full support of the head and the class teachers, the two set about an audit of the school library for books with positive images of people of other races and with handicapped children in interesting roles. Over several terms they did a variety of things. They introduced different costumes such as saris and various African print fabrics into the dressing up box. They had added extras like beads, sequins and pasta in the box on the collage table. They found tapes of African and Asian music. They varied the content of the sandwiches at snack time. They turned the playhouse into a pizza restaurant, and the wheeled vehicles into take-away delivery bikes. They sang 'Frère Jacques' as well as 'Five little sausages'. They talked about holiday locations their friends had been to. The library helped with some artefact collections and book lists. They borrowed artefacts from the LEA collection. The teachers had not stopped to think of the different ways in which they could introduce different cultural ideas without being 'in the face' about it to the parents. The result of the audit of the library had been a shock, and all staff set about introducing more variety when ordering new stock.

Local government areas

The catchment area of the school will also be set in wider context of an administrative area. The old county boundaries determine some areas, but others have a different history. Local education authorities (LEAs) can vary considerably, and not only in size and philosophy. Rutland is so small it only has one secondary school in the authority. Essex, not the biggest authority, has about 80 secondary schools. Some authorities are relatively new, like the unitaries. All are now inspected by the Office for Standards in Education (Ofsted). The way in which the LEA operates may affect your work as an HLTA. It can affect the way in which the total school funding is distributed. Some authorities hold back more, so the actual amount per pupil in the school budget differs. Some schools have had a fully delegated budget and local management for well over ten years, others are still coming to terms with such management. Some authorities still run a TA team, which is bought into by schools, provides opportunities for training for all staff, has strong links to local FE and HE colleges and pay structures and career pathways in place. The recent Unison survey gives an idea of the range of support available to schools in England (Unison 2004).

Health authorities do not even operate over the same geographical areas as other authorities and more autonomy is being given to the primary care trusts anyway. Social services and education are being merged in some areas as the recommendations of *Every Child Matters* are being taken on board.

Local guidance and opportunities therefore vary. It is not possible to say here how you can find further information on how your local authority interprets the government legal framework. You will need to go to one of the senior managers in the school and find out their system for keeping up to date. Some authorities run a sophisticated Intranet with passwords available to certain school staff. This enables these people to download guidance, access documents, talk with advisers or colleagues from other schools in a secure way. Some schools, such as independent schools or a few foundation schools may have their own system of communication.

National legislation, accountability and recommendations

You do not want to burden yourself with vast amounts of things to read. You do not need the fine detail; that is what the senior staff need. They can access a document called *Spectrum*, online which updates readers on changes in legislation, and what documents are newly available, including consultations and announcements of intentions. Some of these will be passed on to relevant staff, put on staff notice boards or referred to in staff newsletters. What you must do is to recognise that these documents exist and how they affect you. Look at how the school interprets the law in its policies.

There are several layers of documents which affect schools. There are acts of parliament – the primary legislation, which are followed up by regulations, statutory instruments and orders which can be made without going back to the Houses of Parliament. Until 2001, the Department for Education and Employment, as it was then, used to send circulars to schools. These were guidance on how schools could or should interpret the law. They now sensibly just call such documents 'guidance'. There are also codes of practice, which although classified strictly as guidance, actually are a bit stronger. If there was an accident, breach of a code would constitute negligence.

There have been various trends over the last few decades. The general values of society or the government in power have been reflected in laws and initiatives affecting school life. Pollard gives a good account of this (Pollard 2002a: 93–5). For instance:

- The child centred movement encouraged teachers to value diversity and individual differences.

- A traditional approach puts emphasis on results and standards.

- A pragmatic stance sees education as purely vocational – training for something later.

- Equal opportunities legislation has:
  - made schools look hard at gender differences in results or class balances;
  - encouraged support for those with SEN;
  - tried to combat things like sexism, racism, homophobia.

- A belief in free market forces brought about local management, and promotes ideas like educational passports or vouchers.

- Human rights legislation has increased the moves towards inclusion.

- The current political scene places a high value on quality within a target orientated, inspectorial culture.

It is easy to see how strong principles held by those in power can influence what is taught to whom, when and how.

The legislation changes all the time. Just take advice and make a mental note of changes. Should you really want further detail, then a useful source book which will be around in school somewhere, is the *Governors' Guide to the Law*, the version depending on the type of school you are in. This lists all the legislation that governors, who are responsible for all that goes on in school, have to take notice of. The websites listed at the end of this chapter will give you more details, and links to yet more sites. Remember, the legislation varies with the sort of school, for instance foundation schools and faith schools will be subject to slightly different rules than community schools. Independent schools will be different again. Note that these distinctions between schools are technical status names for schools and not necessarily the name by which your school is known locally. This status determines the funding strategies and legal framework under which the school operates. Also remember educational traditions, legislation and initiatives are often different in England, Scotland, Wales and Northern Ireland.

Workforce remodelling

This is possibly the most important or difficult challenge facing schools in the next twelve months. This legislation resulted from a teacher workload study (PricewaterhouseCoopers 2001). Later that year, Estelle Morris, the then Secretary of State for Education promised reform (Morris 2001). The series of publications *Time for Standards* (DfES 2002b) along with the publication of the HLTA standards described the way forward. The government has put considerable funding into the initiatives, including the training and assessment procedures for HLTAs. The premise is that qualified teachers are too precious a resource to spend on doing tasks which other people can do as well if not better. These tasks are specialisms in their own right – administration, finance management, behaviour management at informal times and cover supervision. However, the growth of such jobs means a rethinking of the staffing structure in many schools. There was a big pilot exercise in 32 schools, Pathfinders, who were given enhanced funding to enable them to experiment with the use of assistants and ICT to support the work of teachers. It produced some ingenious solutions, but of course, the extra funding means that many schools cannot easily take up the ideas without radical change elsewhere.

The ideas have been contentious because of the suggestions that teachers might be able to take groups of 60 pupils or more, or that so-called unqualified people (HLTAs) should take whole classes. The promise of non-contact time for teachers in primary schools, where none has been available before, is a bold move. These ideas are considered by some, as detrimental to pupils' learning and causing possible teacher redundancies. Some interesting case studies are emerging, where there is no extra funding, and you may well be part of one. There is a lot of material on the workforce remodelling website. Managers and staff of all categories are finding it challenging to rethink the purpose of adults in the school workplace, the tradition of 20 or 30 pupils to one teacher being long entrenched as the norm. Parents have often opted for private rather than state education in the past because of low pupil/teacher ratios regardless of the efficiency or efficacy of this.

The funding has allowed the creation of a national Workforce Remodelling Team, who have trained LEA advisers who in their turn have been training heads, senior managers and governors in the new legislation. Basically, the principles are that teachers, including headteachers, should have an appropriate workload for their job description. Talents and qualifications other than Qualified Teacher Status (QTS) should be recognised and utilised to their best purpose. This has been spelt out in two main regulations. The first bans teachers from 25 administrative tasks – sometimes referred to as 24 or 21 depending on what literature or speaker is providing the information. The other, from September 2005, insists that teachers have 10 per cent of their teaching time as non-pupil contact time – referred to as Planning Preparation and Assessment (PPA) time. From September 2004, no class teacher should undertake more than 38 hours of supply cover a year.

Many schools have set up workforce remodelling teams to look into the various ways of implementing this legislation. The teams may consist of the head, a senior teacher, the bursar, a TA and a governor. It requires a lot of time to consider and consult all of those who may be affected, and hopefully to look more closely at what the actual requirements of the curriculum and the pupils are. The result could be a back-to-square-one scenario where all the school jobs are redefined, and all staff have to reapply for a new job. Redundancies and retraining could result. Hence the extreme sensitivity of the whole process. Where schools have taken this radical look at the needs of the school first, and the climate of the school has encouraged debate and experimentation, there are some interesting solutions being put forward. If you are part of such a reorganisation, you will have found aspects that are worrying as contracts are renegotiated, where potential redundancies loom or hours get cut, and other aspects that are exciting as opportunities for training and development appear and talents are recognised. This process will affect all support staff, technicians and administrative staff as well as teachers. Do have your say, but try to see the whole picture in the school, how pupils' learning may improve and not just how this affects you.

One situation that is appearing, is where one or more TA is employed as an HLTA just to cover classes and employed as an 'ordinary' TA at other times. If this is suggested to you consider it very carefully. Being an HLTA is a holistic thing and not something that can be put on and off. If you accept the job description for an HLTA being put forward in your authority, look closely at the standards and the conditions of service being suggested. You will find that the planning, preparation, delivery, assessment, record keeping and associated tasks are going to take more than just class contact time.

Examples of remodelling

A primary school with over 500 pupils on roll had a floating deputy headteacher, two senior teachers one of whom was the SENCO, also floating and the other had class responsibility, 17 class teachers and 14 part time TAs. (Remember full time means a contract which covers at least 32.5 hours a week for 52 weeks a year not pupil contact time for term time only!) All of the TAs were line managed by the SENCO and concentrated on areas of SEN. After a consultation of teaching staff and governors and various suggestions, the teaching staff accepted that the needs of the curriculum in Key Stages 1 and 2 really demanded some locally based leadership, as did the early years/reception classes. A remodelled senior structure was suggested, whereby two assistant head teachers, one for each key stage and a senior member of staff for the foundation stage – all to be class teachers with time allowed for increased responsibilities were proposed. The SENCO post was to be redefined to include less IEP writing and some whole class teaching on a regular supply type basis. The class teachers were to take much more responsibility for IEPs, with the help of a newly appointed HLTA for their key stage. The SENCO would be a much more advisory role for all staff and to be renamed an inclusion coordinator. There would be no deputy head.

This all meant a reduction in the total teacher numbers, but this was solved by an older member of staff taking voluntary redundancy. The rest of the staff had to apply for the new posts as they wished. This process released budget for three full time HLTAs, one each to work closely with each of the three team leaders and the SENCO (inclusion coordinator), and to manage the key stage team of TAs. The distribution of TA support would be at various levels depending on the spread of pupils with SEN and the needs of the curriculum. This was going to result in some retraining for some TAs, used only to working with one child but they were, as ever, keen to undertake this. One TA was already studying for a TA foundation degree, one was an NNEB and a third was specialising in ICT support. They applied for the HLTA posts when they were advertised among the staff.

A secondary school, with a team of 20 SEN TAs decided to train three or four TAs who were willing, to become generalist TAs and to change their line management from the SENCO to one of the deputy heads. Four TAs were interested in changing. So, the deputy head, as part of his part of his management targets liaised with the department heads to ensure they were happy with the arrangement and could induct the TAs appropriately and include them in their departmental meetings and training. It was agreed with all parties that one would be allotted to each of the core subject departments and one to ICT. The TAs were happy with this and had to be prepared to take classes if necessary. When workforce remodelling came along, with the HLTA status possibilities, the curriculum TAs agreed to undertake assessment. Other TAs became interested in being more generalist. After discussions with the SENCO it was agreed that a regular review of the balance between SEN TAs, (to be called LSAs) and the generalist TAs would be necessary. The HLTA in each department would also develop line management responsibilities. Other departments have become interested in the possibilities of having a dedicated TA for their subject area.

The exercises will not be once and for all. The numbers on roll will fluctuate, affecting the budget by several thousands of pounds per pupil. The need and budget for SEN designated TAs will fluctuate. Capital expenditure on vital repairs could make a big hole in the budget.

The introduction of HLTA status has been much more defined in law than the previous stages of TA development, probably because of the nearness of the status to that of a qualified teacher. The regulations specify that certain activities can only be carried out by qualified teachers or those who satisfy the requirements in the regulations – such as student teachers and instructors with special qualifications and experience. The activities specified are planning, preparation and delivery of lessons, assessing and reporting on the progress development and attainment of pupils. Other people may carry out this specified work in a school if they are supported by a qualified or nominated teacher. They are subject to direction and supervision, in accordance with the school arrangements and provided the head teacher is satisfied they have the skills, expertise and experience to carry out the work. The regulations ask the head teacher to take note of the HLTA standards and LEA guidance on contractual matters. They are also very clear that the purpose of the changes is not to undermine teachers. These are still the lead contributors to teaching and learning and retain accountability for the overall learning outcomes. Teachers and HLTAs are not interchangeable but should complement each other and improve adult:pupil ratios. Time for joint planning and discussion outside pupil contact time but within contracted hours should be built in.

The National Curriculum

The introduction of the NC in 1987 had a profound effect on most state schools and many independent schools. For the first time 'what' to teach became a legal requirement. There was a specific set of subjects, and an entitlement for all children to be taught these subjects. Until that date it was up to each school to determine what was taught and so it was pot luck if you were taught science in primary schools or woodwork in a secondary school. Special schools tended particularly to have a limited curriculum, concentrating on literacy and numeracy. Topic or project work, where all teaching revolved round ideas set by the teacher was common. National assessment procedures were also introduced and Ofsted was set up to ensure the new regulations were being adhered to. Some schools retained the topic approach, and managed to include many subjects within a theme and thus retain coherence to what the pupils received. For some teachers, the programmes of study meant a great overhaul of their own understanding, particularly areas such as science for primary and special school teachers. For some pupils, a breadth of possibilities opened up as they experienced subjects or aspects of subjects not taught before. It entailed a lot of expenditure on equipment and time on in-service training.

Understanding the National Curriculum

- Make sure you have your own copy of the NC if you do not already have it, for the age range with which you work.

- Ensure you are familiar with the requirements for any subject [2.1–2.3] where you may be involved in teaching, whether it is small groups, or larger classes [3.3]. This is particularly true in secondary schools.

- Ascertain whether there are any textbooks or strategies or courses which are commonly used by the teacher or department in which you are placed and discuss relevant pages with one of the teachers.

- If you have doubts consider whether you should attend a course yourself in the local FE college and study for a GCSE in the subject you feel most vulnerable about.

(This book cannot begin to address the curriculum content; you will need to take a proper class lesson in it.)

Strategies

The introduction of the literacy and numeracy strategies to primary schools from 1997 onwards has resulted in considerable changes in how subjects are taught in many schools. The thematic or topic approach has virtually disappeared from many primary schools. Subjects have increasingly been taught in discrete timetabled lessons similar to the secondary model, although some Key Stage 1 teachers are reverting to timetables where several subjects are running concurrently enabling groups to be doing different things. The use of TAs and other adults to support practical group work has assisted this development. It is not new and used to be called an 'integrated day' approach in the 1970s. The success of the strategies in specifying a hierarchical scheme of work for teachers, associated planning grids, and considerable training and resources associated with them encouraged the introduction of a Key Stage 3 strategy for secondary schools which has included science. You may have used a lot of the materials associated with these strategies and taken additional literacy sessions or catch-up groups.

If you are in a primary school make sure you also read the recent primary strategy (DfES 2003c) in order to reinforce the point that the strategies are tools, not legal straitjackets. Enjoyment and creativity must also be considered.

Understanding the strategies

- Make sure you get your own copies of the relevant bits of the strategies for the age group or subjects that you are involved with.

- Make sure you read *Excellence and Enjoyment* (DfES 2003c) whatever key stage you work in.

- Become familiar with the language and the planning formats used by the school.

- How does the school ascertain whether pupils have learnt anything [2.3]?

- Attend any meetings or courses associated with the strategy which could be relevant.

- Discuss the use of the strategy documents in your school with the lead member of staff for the subject – English, mathematics or science.

- Consider the implications of the primary strategy with your mentor teacher. Could its principles apply in secondary schools?

- Access the teachernet, standards and curriculum websites to see what additional materials are available. These are generally downloadable.

Syllabuses and schemes of work

These are not legal requirements but most schools have these in place. Nationally available schemes of work have been written for all the subjects, not just those covered by the strategies and are available from the QCA website. Some schools have adopted these nationally available schemes and just use them but most schools have made minor or major adaptations to them so that they suit their own circumstances. For instance, if the school is near a wildlife centre or an ancient monument or a manufacturing industry it makes every sense to build visits to or visitors from such local resources into the scheme for that school. Small rural schools with mixed age classes need to adapt the scheme to suit. The legal requirement is for coverage of the NC programme of study and the assessment of it using the levels of the attainment targets, not for the coverage of a particular scheme, or strategy. These are the basis for inspection judgements. However, if the requirements are not being met, and the nationally produced materials are being ignored, then there are clearly problems which inspection will pick up. The school will be required to deal with the issues and incorporate action into their action plan or SDP.

In secondary schools, the examination boards' requirements tend to dominate the curriculum and teachers have for many years written syllabuses to match these requirements as well as fulfil the NC requirements. These syllabuses tend to be rather rigid. Each week's lessons being determined in advance, regardless of whether the pupils have understood or even been present. It is possibly here that TAs have been used, to enable students to keep up or catch up if they have missed lessons. It has been the role of some secondary TAs to undertake the differentiation of tasks and lessons to enable those less able to understand. This is despite the fact that they might not have had training for this or have sufficient subject knowledge. HLTA status means that your understanding of the curriculum, syllabus and scheme requirements is much more obvious, and skills you may have gained through osmosis are recognised.

Accountability

Teachers have many legal responsibilities built into their *Schoolteachers' Pay and Conditions*. This is an Act which is updated each year. It covers their responsibilities for learning – for planning preparation, delivery, and assessing and reporting progress; for care – giving guidance and advice, health and safety; for discipline – behaviour management; for communication and management responsibilities including with parents; for their own development including attendance at meetings and reflection. There are no similar conditions laid down for you, as you will be working under the direction of qualified teachers. They take responsibility for what you do. However, this cannot release you from your obligations. Obviously you are going to take responsibility for what you do, particularly in the area of having a 'duty of care, supervision and the avoidance of negligence'. This can be for one pupil or many, if you are 'in charge' for any amount of time.

We live in litigious times and it is tempting just to avoid the issues and not agree to do certain things, as some teachers have with external visits. But if you are going to fulfil your potential and show you can perform to the HLTA status, you must have due regard for the implications. This duty of care is influenced by the age and stage of the pupils, their abilities and needs and how many there are. You have to act 'reasonably' and the onus of proof of negligence is on the complainant. Precedence is established by case law. The school should not put pressure on you to do anything you feel uncomfortable about without appropriate training and support. Do follow the school policies at all times, with regard to disciplinary matters. Always ask for help if you find yourself struggling.

Curriculum accountability is largely determined through a system of assessment, testing, record keeping and data handling depending on the school systems. Certain tests have to be done according to national guidelines like the Standards Assessment Tasks or Tests (SATs), at 11 and 13 years of age. It seems likely at the time of writing that SATs at seven years of age are becoming optional. The results of tests at 11 are published in league tables, as are the results of any nationally taken examinations of students at 16. Most schools back up these legal requirements with banks of tests and procedures at least at the end of each academic year, and in some subjects much more frequently. The Tomlinson report suggested that the examination structure for 14 to 18 year olds could change, with less emphasis on external examinations at 16. The report suggested a four level diploma system, to include basic skills, vocational qualifications and higher A* and A** grade A levels. However, this is unlikely to become accepted.

Inspection

Inspection is a national requirement and the reports are also published for each school. The framework for inspection is also published and you should have a closer look at this. Proposals for changes to start in September 2005 have been put forward after consultation and trial (DfES and Ofsted 2004). Inspection will cover the same areas as now, but will take into account the five areas from *Every Child Matters*. The actual inspections will be shorter and more frequent. They will depend a lot on numerical data from the school testing procedures and a self-evaluation produced by the school. Many schools have already undertaken self-evaluation, using the existing inspection framework as a guide. The guidance handbooks are fairly readable, although the best way is to access just a few pages at a time.

Take the following list. It is the basic structure of a current inspection.

Structure of the evaluation schedule

Effectiveness of the school

1 How successful is the school?

2 What should the school do to improve?

Standards achieved by pupils

3.1 How high are the standards achieved in the areas of learning and subjects of the curriculum?

3.2 How well are pupils' attitudes, values and other personal qualities developed?

Quality of education provided by the school

4 How effective are teaching and learning?

5 How well does the curriculum meet pupils' needs?

6 How well are pupils cared for, guided and supported?

7 How well does the school work in partnership with parents, other schools and the community?

Leadership and management of the school

8 How well is the school led and managed?

9 How good is the quality of education in areas of learning and subjects?

10 What is the quality of other specified features? (Ofsted 2003)

The guidance follows this structure as does the full report of an inspection.

Find the pages in the handbook about one of the sections

You will find each section begins with what the inspectors must evaluate and report on followed by a list of things for inspectors to consider. This in turn will be followed first by a description of what the inspection should focus on and how the inspector should form judgements. These are then followed by a whole lot of questions, printed in bold which the inspectors should use. Each question is followed by statements and descriptions of why this is important and what kinds of things inspectors will see. There are then grids with the descriptors of what constitutes Excellent (1) through to Very Poor (7) practice. For instance if you want to know how inspectors decide whether teaching and learning is good or not, look at where this is described, page 62 in the *Handbook for Inspecting Primary and Nursery Schools* (Ofsted 2003). These judgements would be the same for teachers or assistants working in a teaching role. Your deployment, effectiveness, guidance and training are all considered in an inspection, see page 68 (Ofsted 2003).

An international dimension

The global nature of our current life generally also affects schools, with international comparisons being made on a regular basis. European legislation also makes itself felt. Food labelling and building regulations for instance are affected by laws made outside our parliament. However most of the items will not affect your work directly, more your role as a human being.

The increased mobility of people means that there are fewer communities with a single ethnic origin. Asylum seekers and economic migrants have come to the British Isles in much greater numbers in the last five to ten years, so that there must be very few schools indeed without one or several pupils who were born in a different country or whose parents were born abroad. The cheapness of air travel has meant many more families travel abroad for their holidays, and our high streets have restaurants with dishes from many different parts of the world. You may well be supporting pupils with a variety of interests and needs greater than ever before. Build on this opportunity to share the variety it will open up.

There is European funding available for people working in the public services, of which education is one, under programmes called Socrates. This will pay for travel to another European country on a week's study programme with people in similar positions from other countries. The funds are managed in this country by the British Council. You might be interested in finding out more about this.

You should consider when it is appropriate and how you introduce some of the important topics for discussion to a class or group of pupils you are working with. Topics like global warming, the meaning of democracy, human rights issues, fair trials can be introduced to even young children in the right context and at the right time. Primary children can get very interested in issues of recycling. Year ones can understand and enjoy representation at the school council and its procedures. All children will be familiar with aspects of fair play and rewards and consequences of actions.

Essential to read

The National Curriculum for your speciality.
The relevant parts of any of the strategies of the key stage in which you work.
DfES (2003c) *Excellence and Enjoyment: A Strategy for Primary Schools* (Advice DfES/ 0377/2003). London: Department for Education and Skills.

Useful websites for further information

www.curriculumonline.gov.uk for curriculum support materials
www.dfes.gov.uk for the latest educational news and links to other sites
www.lg-employers.gov.uk for information about national occupational standards and general advice for support staff
www.nc.uk.net for curriculum information and support materials for inclusion, SEN and G&T
www.ngfl.gov.uk for a general gateway to educational resource
www.qca.org.uk for support materials especially schemes of work and assessment information
www.remodelling.org for up to date information and details about the workforce remodelling initiative
www.teachernet.gov.uk for support materials and documents
www.teachernet.gov.uk/teachingassistants for general information for TAs
www.tta.gov.uk/hlta for general information about and for HLTAs
www.standards.dfes.gov.uk for statistics and strategy materials
your local LEA website

A possible useful guide for legal information which will be in your school somewhere is: *A Guide to the Law for School Governors* from the DfES. The edition will depend on the status of your school.

Inspection guidance can be informative but should not be your sole indicator of good practice. Find what else your school uses.

Personal reflection and development

Personal development

Continuing profession development is important whatever occupation you are in. In the past, one of the reasons that TAs were invisible, was the way in which they were expected to understand their role through a process of osmosis, to absorb what they were to do and how they were to behave through some sort of innate skill. It was assumed that the tasks you were asked to do were basic. Anyone with an ounce of sense could do them. Anyone who had been a parent, as most TAs were, had at least two ounces of sense and one of those was about the needs of children. Luckily most TAs not only enjoyed their jobs but wanted to do their best, and get better. If assisting teaching and learning is to be taken seriously, and over the last six years it has been, depending on this quality is not enough. One of the standards [1.6] actually spells out the need for continuing your own development.

Whatever you decide to do in the future, standard 1.6 is important, even if you decide working at this higher level is not for you. If you have just started or are at any of the intermediate levels, you must continue to aim to improve your own practice. If you go on to take a full degree or higher professional training, it is vital. Any activity in life is fuller if you aim to improve it, observe what happens, think about it and talk about it with friends and colleagues. It is the old 'plan, do, review' cycle.

Observation

This is the first skill you develop when working in a school. This is how you learnt how the school operated when you started as a TA. You watched what other people did, especially the teachers, and you took their actions and behaviour as the accepted mode of working in the school. Even where you have been lucky to have a full induction process, you will still have watched how other people did things. You also watched the pupils in your care, how they reacted to the teacher, to their friends and how they reacted to you. It was from these, often unrealised, observations that you have built up your experience base and honed your own skills. It is by making more structured observations with a focus, and discussing and reflecting on it that you will develop even further.

However, it is also important to recognise that all members of staff have a duty of confidentiality about all that they see, hear and read while in school. It is another facet of professionalism. It is not just a matter of remembering not to chat in the local shop or

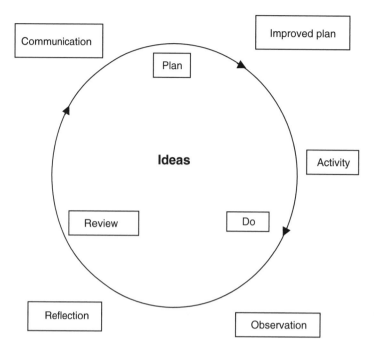

Figure 7.1   The investigative process cycle

not to share a juicy bit of gossip with your best friend. Do remember, if you are writing anything for your TA courses, that all names should be changed or coded so that anyone mentioned becomes anonymous. All photography and videoing is very sensitive these days and must only be done with the full permission of the school management and the parents and young people concerned, using proper protocols. Photographs are acceptable evidence for HLTA assessment, provided they remain in the school.

There are suggestions for ways of observing in many books. Wragg's book on classroom observation has all the kinds of examples you might want (Wragg 1994). If you have done any TA courses, the DfES induction package or those leading to NVQ or similar, you will have done observation on individual pupils. Pages 39–42 in *Assisting Learning and Supporting Teaching* gives some starter suggestions on observation to follow, if you have not done a course (Watkinson 2002).

Just be sure to remember the protocols you need to follow when doing any kind of formal observation.

Possible protocols to consider for classroom observation

The following needs to be discussed between the TA and the class teacher where any observation is to take place:

- The purpose of the exercise is to . . . e.g. understand more about . . .
- The adults involved will be . . .
- The pupils involved will be . . .

The head teacher/department head/line manager has been told what is happening, and has agreed.

It needs to be checked that:

- anything written was to be shared first with each other so that comments can be made and points of accuracy checked;

- any comments to be seen by others will be anonymised, or amalgamated with others to preserve confidentiality;

- the main audience of any summary written material would be . . . e.g. the other member of a course, or an outside reader;

- the people observed or interviewed can have a copy of the notes made if they so wished;

- you know what will happen to any written records;

- the intended outcome of the activity is . . .

- you know what you will do if the observation shows up anything within the classroom or school that someone wishes to address or celebrate;

- if others get involved, they would be covered by the same sort of protocols;

- someone seeks permission of the parents of the children closely involved.

Either side should be able to make comment at any time in the process if there is any discomfort or suggestion about what is taking place or being said. (Watkinson 2002: 39–40)

Another thing to remember is that your act of observation may change what is happening. If pupils see you writing or using a camera they could immediately behave differently. This is less likely to happen if you do this regularly or other adults are also in the habit of observing them. The role of the observer – inspector, assessor, trainee teacher or TA or appraiser may also influence the process.

While you are in training you should take the opportunity to do some structured observations of what is going on in the class.

Looking at group dynamics

Ask for a time to observe a group at work on a collaborative task or playing.

Draw a map of where each member of the group is standing or sitting.

Then for a period of ten minutes or quarter of an hour

either: make a list of members and tally when each member speaks, or: draw a line on your map each time someone speaks showing the line of communication,

or: tape-record the conversation, noting who is speaking each time so that you can transcribe the tape later,

or: look out for all the incidents of non-verbal communication.

Did any one person dominate? Why?

Did anyone not contribute at all? Why?

Was there any off-task activity or discussion? Why?

Did any outside things influence what was going on?

Did it matter where the group members were placed?

Did the group break into any sub-groups? Why? Did it help the task?

What sort of intervention, if any, would have made things work better?

Was it an appropriate activity for group work? (Watkinson 2003c: 27–8)

Observing whole class dynamics

You can use quantitative methods – using numbers that can be counted and displayed as graphs or in statistics – or qualitative methods, noting down in words what you see happening. The two methods can be combined where you note words against a time scale, or tally the number of times a particular action happens.

Do ensure you talk with the teacher first before doing this kind of observation! You will need to follow proper protocols both with the teacher and regarding any pupils you are observing.

1 A well known way of doing this for a large number is to use the Flanders Interaction Analysis Category (FIAC) system. Simply, this is a grid with minutes on one axis, the horizontal one, and the categories that you want to observe on the other. Marks are made in the minute squares every three seconds to record what is happening. It needs refining to show what you are particularly interested in but the grid principle can be adapted to observe pupils rather than categories or any combination of two variables that you want. Classroom dynamics are so complex, that a mixture of quantitative and qualitative methods is needed to get anywhere near understanding what is going on. Limit your ideas and focus on something like noting who the teacher is talking to every half minute, or which pupils answer questions or put their hand up or are off task.

2 A different approach is to draw a simple map of the classroom, with tables and chairs as simple blocks. Number the chairs and have a key showing who is sitting where at the beginning of the lesson. Photocopy the map so that you have several copies. Note the

time on the first sheet and just draw the movements of any pupils as lines. Change the sheet, say, every five minutes – it will depend on the mobility of the class being observed – noting the time spent on each sheet. At the end you will have a record of who is out of their seat the most, and what they were actually doing.

3 Recording actual conversations using a tape recorder is possible but incredibly time consuming in terms of making transcripts. Analysing the end result is also difficult. It is probably of more use to note what kinds of conversation are going on, whether they are on task, who talks and when, who dominates and who rarely speaks. Recording teacher–pupil interactions can be very illuminating as to where the teacher is actually spending his or her time. Any detail as to whether the teacher is asking a question, dealing with disruption or giving instructions can increase the usefulness of the information. You can see how important it is to do such observations with the permission and understanding of the teacher you are observing!

Do talk all your observations through with the teacher in whose class you were afterwards, and deal with the records you have made appropriately.

When you start taking a class and gain your confidence, try getting someone to do similar observations on you.

Hopefully, you will be observed anyway as part of your annual appraisal.

Photograph 7.1 Being observed watching children at work

Evaluation

It is relatively easy to observe, write down what you see, provided you have a limited focus. Trying to write it all down is hopeless. The next step is to analyse what you did see.

One of the difficult questions for you will be 'how do I know what is important and what is not?' This is where you need information from outside of yourself. This is the purpose

Analysis and evaluation

- What did I focus on? What did I think I would see?
- Did the practical arrangements I made work out?
- How can I make any sense of what I have seen?
- Is there any background information that will help me understand?
- Was it unusual or a snapshot of something that happens every day or every lesson?
- Did anything surprise me?
- Why did it happen?
- Was it important or irrelevant? How do you know?
- How did it happen? Could you do the same thing?
- What might happen next?
- What happened before the time you observed that helped it happen? Was anybody else involved?
- Could different things have happened if different people or pupils had been there or different resources had been used?
- Do I need to do it again? In the same way or differently?

Then you should be able to answer:

- Have I learnt anything from doing this observation?
- Was there any value in it?

And then:

- What are you going to do with all the thoughts you have had about the observation?
- Does it make any difference to the way you do things in the future?
- Do you need to talk about what you saw to others?

of any course you are on, or extra reading that you do, to give you more information. It may be about curriculum knowledge, or process skills or descriptions of emotional states or acceptable behaviour patterns. This will all give you ideas of what is of value, to give you yardsticks to measure or assess by. Your first structured observations may have been at the behest of the teacher to assess who listens at the beginning of lessons and who doesn't. You would have ended up with a grid of pupils' names and a time frame. You could just hand this to the teacher and think no more. But then reflect on the observations. For instance it may be that:

- the topic is boring – but because it is a repeat of something done yesterday;
- the teacher has a cold and her voice was in a monotone sending the class to sleep;

- the class have just come in from lunch and would really like to have a quiet nap;

- the subject matter was far to difficult or far too easy;

- the range of pupils paying attention was not the group the teacher anticipated;

- it went on too long, the earlier stages were OK;

- some of those apparently not listening may well have done so, or those looking alert may have been thinking of something else.

Further reflection

Then if you know what the learning objectives were and you reflected further you might begin to think:

- How can you tell what is happening in another's brain?

- How could you find out later who was taking in information from the teacher?

- Could visual aids have helped make it interesting?

- Explaining why the talk had to come before the activity might have helped.

Reflection on the process and having more information about the subject will help you make much more of the observation.

Discussion

Reflecting on your own is important, but sharing those thoughts with others can extend the value of them even further.

Take the above example:

Talk with the teacher to find out why he or she wanted the observation done in the first place.

- What is the background information?
Ask the pupils themselves why they behaved in the way they did.

- Was it a heavy lunch?

- Was the room too warm?

- Had the supply teacher covered the same ground the day before?

- Could they remember more than was obvious from your observation?

- Are there any resources or aids that could help similar lessons in the future?

- Would repeat observations show up patterns of inattention in certain pupils that needs dealing with?

Discussion with colleagues in the school, with the pupils themselves, or with colleagues on a course or at a meeting can all help to give added dimensions to your own thoughts. This discussion may result in action which creates real improvement for the pupils and their learning as well as your own learning.

Reflective practice

Get into the habit of reflecting as many aspects of your work as you can. After a day's work, think about it on the way home or in the bath. Don't dwell on it for a long time. If there was something you want to remember jot it down. Don't keep on thinking about it or you will not sleep. It is important to give yourself personal space, and give your family and other activities attention and time.

There is a simple but helpful little rhyme by Rudyard Kipling from the *Just-so Stories* which is worth remembering:

> I keep six honest serving-men
> (They taught me all I knew);
> Their names are What and Why and When
> And How and Where and Who.

Working with children at this higher level is not just doing what you are told or even just 'doing'. You need to know why you do it in the first place and after the event what you have learnt from it not just what the pupils have learnt. Of course, you do not do a deep or written analysis after every lesson or every day. One of the problems with an occupation like teaching is that you do not walk away from the job at the end of the day. Thoughts just go on revolving round your head. This can lead you to become obsessive, and spend too much time searching after perfection. Watch out for this, for while reflective practice is essential, and to some extent unavoidable, it should be controlled and channelled. Have a regular time when you read around or about your work, when you study or prepare. Have a small notebook in your bag to jot ideas or thoughts down, and then forget them until your study time. Keep a small notebook by the bed if you get into a habit of waking up with ideas – jot them down and go back to sleep!

Remember theory and practice come together. Even in the research world, observation of some kind is usually the precursor to investigation. Reflection on the observation leads to more ideas and the theories build up. This leads to more observation and investigation. Even a researcher given a project to follow or a question to investigate will base their work on previous experience. Education research has been criticised for being divorced from the classroom, carried out by people in universities not schools. Some research is called action research, where practitioners – teachers – investigate a problem directly relevant to them in their own schools to find ways to improve their own teaching or the learning of pupils in their own school. Your reflective practice is just the beginning. It is also worth finding out whether someone has already investigated some of the points you may be interested in. Try putting your area of interest into an educational library website and see what comes up.

Alongside your observations and ideas you will need to read. If you are on a course, the tutor may be able to help you, point you in the direction of a book or journal that has an article about your area of interest. You may have tried some of those listed at the end of chapters in this book. After reading a passage in an educational type book, think about whether it has anything to say to you and the way in which you work. Do not mark the pages unless you own the book. Post-its can provide useful temporary markers. Use them with care in borrowed books. They can leave a sticky trace when you remove them. Make a note of any interesting thoughts, or quotable bits, making sure you also note the author's name, the date and place of publication, and the publisher as well as the title. Do not forget the page reference of any quote you record. See the way in which the references are detailed in this book for help in adding any reference to your own assignments if you do them.

Don't think you have to read such a book from beginning to end.

Find a title in a library or a shop

Look at the list of contents, if this appeals and seems to fit what you are interested in.

Read the summary and conclusions (probably in the first chapter and the last).

Pick a chapter that seems most interesting.

    Again read the introduction and the conclusion to the chapter.

Look quickly at any diagrams or pictures.

If it still appeals, borrow it or buy it.

Read the detail.

Make notes as you go if something strikes you.

When you read, reflect on the content:

- Does it ring true to what you know and have experienced?
- Does it offer useful suggestions which you could try out?
- Do you want to share some of the ideas with other people?
- Does it change any of your ideas?
- What can you do about it?

After a session on a course, don't just accept what the tutor has said; think about it. Ask questions of the information and experiences you have had in the same way as those suggested about an observation. It is not just the 'what' that is important.

Keep a modest diary. You will find this invaluable when you come to do your HLTA assessments and for later reference. I do not mean a daily account of your activities, but a collection of dated reflections on your work. Keep a pad of file paper handy. A5 is quite sufficient, or A4 if you wish. If something happens when you are working which stays in your mind, or you want to remember, put it down, and add time, day and place. Be very careful about naming anybody in such a diary, always try to change the names. Collect the jottings in a small ringbinder. Then you can refer to this when you need evidence for any course. Just highlight the entry and put the standard number alongside the entry in another colour, say red. Look at the guidance for the standards and you will see all the examples could have come from such a diary.

Try searching on the Internet, but beware, anyone can put material on the Internet. Journals and books have all been vetted before publication to try to ensure that the content is reliable and valid, not a practical joke, a crazy idea or even just very biased. Remember, just because somebody has got into print, they do not necessarily have all the right answers even if it has been vetted. But the Internet is unpoliced, except for pornography, viruses and spam.

Browse the magazines in the staffroom, including the *Times Educational Supplement*. TAs do submit letters to this from time to time which get published. It carries articles of interest to teachers and includes regular supplements with practical resources you might find useful. It has regular features for newly qualified teachers and governors but not for TAs – maybe there is an opening for you? Ask the teachers you work with what magazines they use, ask to borrow some and see if they interest you. There are specialist magazines for SEN, early years like *Nursery World*, and various key stages – like *Child Education* for Key Stage 1 and *Junior Education* for Key Stage 2.

Consider membership of a curriculum or SEN association as well as a union. They provide their own in-house magazines, conferences and specialist support and information. For instance, the Association for Science Education (ASE), the biggest subject association, has membership for TAs, technicians, teachers and lecturers interested in science in schools. It has specialist committees, magazines and many useful publications. Try its website for further information. Ask your teachers about their subject and how they keep up to date. Try the other subject association websites, wherever your interest lies.

It is important that you try to visit other schools, discuss with their TAs or teachers what expectations they have of their pupils in educational and behavioural terms and how this can affect outcomes, both measurable and the less substantial longer-term ones like attitudes to the world around them. All schools are different, not just in their physical layout, but their philosophy and practices.

Reflection may not lead to immediate changes but it will lead you to greater insights into what you do. Finding this out for yourself is more important than being told how to behave or what to do. In the long term your practice will improve. You will be more knowledgeable, interested and effective in supporting pupils' learning. At the very least you will get more satisfaction from your job.

Your development and future

HLTA status

If you are reading this book, you already are considering the way in which you do your job. I doubt that you are considering HLTA status just to get a pay rise for something you are

Some examples of reflective practice in the early years of TAs

Pairs of teachers and TAs from both secondary and primary phases came on a two-day course on teaching and learning. The TAs were not highly qualified. Between the two days the pair were asked to use a focused observation technique to look at something in their joint classroom and share their observations. They looked at:

> Group work in science and maths
> Individuals working on their own and within groups
> Groups inside and outside the classroom
> Pupils during quiet reading time
> Pupils discussing ideas around the earth and the sun
> Handwriting practice.

One TA interviewed the group of pupils afterwards as well.

The results were reported back to the group on the second day of the course and discussed by the group.

Several generalisations were possible from their individual findings:

- Children need to be on their own at times not always supported by an adult, including those children with SEN.
- Familiarity with an adult can be detrimental as well as helpful. Help can be rejected.
- Non verbal gestures – the smile, the nod or a listening mode can be as active in supporting learning as verbal communication.
- The ownership of the activity is the teacher's. They know the purpose and where it could lead. TAs keep children on task, enabling them to complete activities, checking avoidance strategies.
- Tasks can be meaningful rather than occupational – talking about a picture rather than just colouring in.
- Where the TA is involved in investigational activity they can make the difference between enjoyable play and measurement and control of variables.
- Intervention – and non-intervention skills, are probably the most crucial of all.
- TAs' questioning can make the children think. Discussions can be facilitated. Ideas can be pulled together.
- Sometimes it may mean taking demanding individuals away from their peers, thus enabling the group to work.
- The importance of communication and dialogue between the partners.
- TAs do instinctively what they feel is the right thing, but want and need guidance and reassurance to make the best use of their knowledge and skill. (Watkinson 1999: 68)

already doing, although that will be part of it. You will be considering where the acquisition of such status will lead and possibly which way you want to get the status.

You have several options, all of which are spelt out clearly on the HLTA website run by the TTA, some of which are still in the development phase. One of your early options is to get hold of or make yourself a spreadsheet with the standards in the first column and two further columns. In the second column put what you know you already do to show that standard – real examples such as you would put in a diary mentioned above. The third column is for you to think what further work you need to do to prove that you can perform at that standard. Note that for some of the standards, the individual parts are required. For others, while they are not required, it is hard to imagine one part being successfully achieved without the other parts.

Table 7.1　A list of standards which have mandatory subsidiary sections

Standard	Sections which must be evidence separately
1.1	They have high expectations of all pupils. They respect their different backgrounds. They are committed to raising their educational achievement.
2.1	They understand their specialist area sufficiently to support pupils' learning. They acquire further knowledge to contribute effectively and with confidence to their classes.
2.4	They know how to use ICT to advance pupils' learning. They use common ICT tools for their own and pupils' benefit.
3.2.3	They monitor pupils' participation and progress then provide feedback to teachers. They monitor pupils' participation and progress then give constructive support to pupils as they learn.
3.3.5	– They advance pupils' learning when working with: – Individual pupils – Small groups – Whole classes where the assigned teacher is not present

Table 7.2　A list of the standards which have subsidiary sections which seem essential to me to show the overall standard

Standards	Sections which may need evidencing separately
1.4	Work collaboratively with colleagues effectively Knowing when to seek help and advice.
2.2	Familiar with the school curriculum, the age-related expectations, teaching methods, testing/examination frameworks
2.3	Understand the aims, content, teaching strategies and intended outcomes of lessons
2.9	Know strategies for purposeful learning environment and promote good behaviour
3.2.2	Monitor pupils' responses to learning tasks and modify their approach
3.2.4	Awareness of record keeping importance Obtaining information Recording strategies Analysis

Continued

Table 7.2 Continued

Standards	Sections which may need evidencing separately
3.3.1	Use clearly structured teaching and learning activities Interest and motivate pupils and advance their learning.
3.3.7	Recognise and respond to equal opportunities issues Challenging stereotyped views, and by challenging bullying and harassment
3.3.8	They organise and manage safely the learning activities, the physical teaching space and the resources for which they are given responsibility

This exercise will help you decide what route is best for you. Do you need more time, experience, training or study? How will you get these? Further details of the training and assessment routes are available on the TTA website, and the funding route is through your Local Education Authority.

The assessment only route assumes that you can fill in all of the second column now, in other words that you are already doing things in school which show evidence of all the standards. The training for the assessment only route is a training for assessment not for being an HLTA. The training providers will brief you on how to fill in the paperwork for an external assessor to look at and what the assessors do when they visit you at school. They will not see you in the classroom, so it will be up to you to show in written evidence that you can fulfil the standards. They will not give an immediate judgement as their report has to go back to the provider to be moderated, and there is national moderation as well. You will be notified of the result from the TTA, who will also give you a registration number, just like teachers get when they qualify. If you fail, you can get further guidance from the provider.

In submitting for assessment the candidate is seeking to demonstrate that they have attained the standards.

In carrying out an assessment the assessor is seeking to prove to the moderators that the judgement is soundly based upon written evidence.

In carrying out moderation the moderator is seeking to prove that the decisions they have come to are correct and soundly based on an audit trail. (Formation 2004: private communication, emphasis in original)

If you feel you are in need of training to do the job, there are 50 day courses, which will include 20 days at a centre with a tutor, time in school and self-study, probably computer assisted. There are also likely to be top-up courses for certain areas of the standards only. You may also feel you would rather go for a foundation degree and get a much fuller training although that will take longer. The TTA are piloting ways to possibly link such courses with gaining HLTA status.

Remember, HLTA status does not confer any automatic right either to a job or a pay rise. If you want to know more about the frameworks being developed over issues of pay and conditions of service, the National Joint Council for Local Government Services, have produced guidance notes for LEAs which can be downloaded from the Employers Organisation website. The document is called *School Support Staff – The way Forward* (NJC 2003). Pay scales will be set locally and job descriptions will be negotiated within your school. Do check yours and the possible changes to it and your conditions of service before making any big decisions about training. However, even if there is no change in your current school, gaining such a status will improve your CV. This would enhance any chances of gaining a job elsewhere or entry to an HE college if applying for further training.

Future directions

Career pathways for TAs are now clear, not easy, but clear. The levels are defined and available on the employers and workforce remodelling websites. Induction training is available in most, if not all, local authorities. Minimum levels of literacy and numeracy are defined and used by some employers and standards, and skills courses to support these are available free from the Learning and Skills Council. The National Occupational Standards are published at levels 2 and 3 and may well be being developed at level 4. The HLTA standards are published and foundation degree courses for TAs are available. Courses matching and supporting these standards are all available, and often at a subsidised or grant-aided rate. Teacher training places are available for those who want to go on full time or part time routes. Teacher qualifications still include graduate status which can be obtained through the various routes.

Foundation degrees mean two years' full time or up to four years' part time study, with assignments and assessment. Remember that you will need at least to have completed a three-year full degree to become a teacher, and the nature of that degree is specified by the TTA. So look on their website for extra information before making your decisions.

All of this assumes you are looking for further accreditation. You may just wish to go on being a very good TA. Great! Whatever you decide do keep on thinking, reading, talking, asking questions and trying to find the answers. Attend any courses offered if the subject seems relevant.

Do keep up a personal, professional portfolio. This can be a ringbinder with details of your educational background, somewhere to keep those certificates – so that you can produce them when asked as you are in proving standard 2.6 – and to keep a record of professional events. You can add as many personal details as you wish.

A personal portfolio

Have dividers in your ringbinder for:

- your personal information and history;
- your place of work and relevant documents;
- your job and how it is going;
- documentation concerning any professional review or appraisals that you have;
- your own notes;

- a record of the course details, dates and outcomes of course, any associated certificates which you want to keep for reference later (if you go on a course, unless there is very little paperwork attached, you will need a separate file for the course materials);

- letters of appreciation or references.

The thin plastic pockets designed for ringfiles are ideal containers for documents like certificates, but notice you will need extra wide dividers if you use these. They overlap A4 pages. (Watkinson 2002: 8)

Going back to the garden analogy, a single bulb planted in the garden may have one or more blooms. Several planted in a clump show up and show off their colour and make you take notice. If schools work together cooperatively in a cluster or consortium they can share expertise and ideas. Why not consider a TA network in your area where you can share your ideas and maybe find other potential HLTAs. Networking of this kind can be really productive in designing your own professional development. Eventually, there must be a national TA network or association where you all share and have a voice. The blooms will be seen when there are enough of them.

Networking

Speak to your line manager or your head.

Ask if the school belongs to a consortium or cluster.

Ask if there are meetings of the heads, subject leaders, governors or SENCOs.

Ask if it would be possible for the school to facilitate the meeting of all the TAs from the cluster in your school.

Consider a speaker, timing and refreshments.

An example

A group of TAs in one primary school had all over a period of several years undertaken the Open University Specialist Teacher Certificate. They did not want to go on to be teachers, but did want to continue their own professional development. The SENCO held regular meetings with them and kept them up to date on legislation, like the changes in the code of practice and discussed individual children's needs and a variety of strategies. One of the TAs thought wider. After approaching the head for permission, she wrote to the heads of the cluster schools inviting their TAs to an evening meeting in their school to talk about a regular group. They put on tea and coffee with biscuits, and asked a local freelance TA tutor to speak. Sixty people turned up. There was discussion about the future, role of unions, what would interest colleagues and some interesting new resources. They agreed to meet in a different school each term and find items of interest. Suggestions ranged from speakers like the local educational psychologist, a local doctor, an LEA officer, to a brains trust and workshops. They had vision of an annual conference, joining up with other local groups if they could find them.

Your life

It is easy to get sucked into a job in a school too much. The very nature of the job, working with children and young people, feeling you can make a difference, can get to you. The picture of the excellent teacher seems to indicate someone who is all singing, all dancing, giving up all their free time to the job and even dreaming about it. However, it is also important to keep a proper life going outside school to ensure you are a rounded person, with interests to contribute. Schools need to be open to reality and life, not enclosed text-book, curriculum bound, ivory towers. Try to keep up hobbies and holidays, enjoying being with your friends and family, watching and reading about your interests as well as educational matters. This is not easy to do if you are also studying on a course and running a family and a home while working, but something to bear in mind when the course finishes. Workforce remodelling is about workload reform as well as standards. Just remember, you need a work/life balance just like the teachers and the head!

Further reading

Bold, C. (2004) 'The reflective practitioner', in Bold C., (ed.) *Supporting Learning and Teaching.* London: David Fulton Publishers, pp. 1–13. An introduction to the ideas of being a reflective practitioner.

Hayes, D. (2003) *Planning, Teaching and Class Management in Primary Schools,* 2nd edn, Chapter 7 – Critical reflection, pp. 109–12. London: David Fulton Publishers.

Pollard, A. (2002a) *Reflective Teaching – Effective and Evidence-Informed Professional Practice.* London and New York: Continuum. Try the final chapters, pp. 387–433.

Pollard, A. (ed.) (2002b) *Readings for Reflective Teaching.* London and New York: Continuum. Some of the readings supporting the above chapters by Solomon and Tresman pp. 353–5, and Archer pp. 363–4, both short extracts from longer works.

Ritchie, C. and Thomas, P. (2004) *Successful Study – Skills for Teaching Assistants.* London: David Fulton Publishers.

Helpful websites

www.dfes.gov.uk/leagateway to find your LEA website

www.hlta.gov.uk and www.tta.gov.uk/hlta for general information about and for HLTAs

www.lg-employers.gov.uk for job descriptions, pay and conditions, and other support staff information

www.lsc.gov.uk for help with English and mathematics qualification training

www.remodelling.org for up to date information and details about the workforce remodelling initiative

www.teach.gov.uk for information on training to be a teacher

www.teach.go.uk for help with routes into teaching

Subject association websites

English: www.nate.org.uk – National Association of Teachers of English
Mathematics: m-a.org.uk and atm.org.uk – Mathematics Association and the Association of Teachers of Mathematics
Science: ase.org.uk – Association for Science Education
Design and technology: data.org.uk – Design and Technology Association

Also useful is the ICT support website: www.becta.org.uk British Educational Communications and Technology Agency, a UK agency supporting ICT developments.

Useful websites

www.curriculumonline.gov.uk for curriculum support materials

www.dfes.gov.uk for the latest educational news and links to other sites

www.dfes.gov.uk/behaviourimprovement/primarypilot/index.cfm – a website to find out more about Sebs

www.dfes.gov.uk/leagateway to find your LEA website

www.fultonpublishers.co.uk for useful books for TAs, teaching and learning and SEN specialisms

www.hlta.gov.uk and www.tta.gov.uk/hlta for general information about and for HLTAs

www.lg-employers.gov.uk for information about national occupational standards and general advice for support staff, job descriptions, pay and conditions, and other support staff information

www.lsc.gov.uk for help with English and mathematics qualification training

www.nc.uk.net for curriculum information and support materials for inclusion, SEN and G&T

www.ngfl.gov.uk for general gateway to educational resources

www.qca.org.uk for support materials especially schemes of work and assessment information

www.remodelling.org for up to date information and details about the workforce remodelling initiative

www.standards.dfes.gov.uk for statistics and strategy materials

www.teach.go.uk for help with routes into teaching

www.teach.gov.uk for information on training to be a teacher

www.teachernet.gov.uk for support materials and documents in general

www.teachernet.gov.uk/teachingassistants for general information for TAs

www.tta.gov.uk/hlta for general information about and for HLTAs

Professional associations or unions being used by TAs

www.unison.org.uk – a union for support staff

www.gmb.org.uk – a union for support staff

www.pat.org.uk – Professionals Allied to Teaching (PAtT): accessible via the Professional Association of Teachers (PAT)

www.napta.org.uk – an association formed by the Pearson Publishing group to provide services to TAs

The main teachers' associations
www.teachers.org.uk for National Association of teachers (NUT)
www.teacherxpress.com for Association of Teachers and Lecturers (ATL)
www.nasuwt.org.uk for National Association of Schoolmasters and Union of Women Teachers (NASUWT)

Subject association websites
English: www.nate.org.uk – National Association of Teachers of English
Mathematics: m-a.org.uk and atm.org.uk – Mathematics Association and the Association of Teachers of Mathematics
Science: ase.ork.uk – Association for Science Education
Design and technology: data.org.uk – Design and Technology Association
Also useful is the ICT support website: www.becta.org.uk – British Educational Communications and technology Agency, a UK agency supporting ICT developments.

References

Armstrong, F., Armstrong, D. and Barton, L. (eds) (2000) *Inclusive Education*. London: David Fulton Publishers.

ASE (1996) *Safeguards in the School Laboratory*, 10th edn. Hatfield: Association for Science Education.

ASE (2001) *Be Safe: Health and Safety in Primary School Science and Technology*. Hatfield: Association for Science Education.

Balshaw, M. (1999) *Help in the Classroom*, 2nd edn. London: David Fulton Publishers.

Balshaw, M. and Farrell, P. (2002) *Teaching Assistants*. London: David Fulton Publishers.

Barrow, A. (2004) 'The changing educational scene', in Bold, C. (ed.) *Supporting Learning and Teaching*, pp. 14–33. London: David Fulton Publishers.

Bastiani, J. (1989) *Working with Parents: A Whole-School Approach*. London: Routledge and NFER-Nelson Publishing Company Limited.

Bastiani, J. (2003) *Materials for Schools: Involving Parents, Raising Achievement*. London: Department for Education and Skills

Ben-Peretz, M. S. S. and Kupermitz, H. (1999) 'The teachers' lounge and its role in improving learning environments in schools', in Freiberg, H. J. (ed.) *School Climate*. London and Philadelphia: Falmer Press.

Bills, L. (2004) 'Working with parents and other adults', in Brooks, V., Abbott, I. and Bills, L. (eds) *Preparing to Teach in Secondary Schools*. Maidenhead and New York: Open University Press with McGraw-Hill Education.

Blamires, M., Robertson, C. and Blamires, J. (1997) *Parent–Teacher Partnership*. London: David Fulton Publishers.

Bold, C. (2004) `The reflective practitioner', in Bold, C. (ed.) *Supporting Learning and Teaching*, pp. 1–13. London: David Fulton Publishers.

Brighouse, T. and Woods, D. (1999) *How to Improve your School*. London and New York: Routledge.

Clarke, C., Boateng, P. and Hodge, M. (2003) *Every Child Matters* (Green Paper CYPUECM). London: Department for Education and Skills.

Cohen, L., Manion, L. and Morrison, K. (2004) *A Guide to Teaching Practice*, 5th edn. London: Routledge Falmer.

Cole, M. (ed.) (2002) *Professional Values and Practice for Teachers and Student Teachers*, 2nd edn. London: David Fulton Publishers.

DATA (1996) *Primary Design and Technology – A Guide for Teacher Assistants*. Wellesbourne: The Design and Technology Association.

DfEE (1996) *Supporting Pupils with Medical Needs in Schools* (Circular 14/96). London: Department for Education and Employment.

DfEE (1998a) *Health and Safety of Pupils on Educational Visits* (HSPV2). London: Department of Education and Employment.

DfEE (1998b) *Guidance on First Aid in Schools* (Good Practice Guide). London: Department for Education and Employment.

DfEE (1998c) *The Use of Force to Control or Restrain Pupils* (Circular 10/98). London: Department for Education and Employment.

DfEE (1999a) *The National Curriculum – Handbook for Primary Teachers in England: Key Stages 1 and 2*. London: Department for Education and Skills and the Qualifications and Assessment Authority.

DfEE (1999b) *The National Curriculum – Handbook for Primary Teachers in England: Key Stages 3 and 4*. London: Department for Education and Skills and the Qualifications and Assessment Authority and the Qualifications and Curriculum Authority.

DfEE (2000) *Bullying – Don't Suffer in Silence* (DfEE 0064 2000). London: Department for Education and Employment.

DfES (2001) *Special Educational Needs Code of Practice*. London: Department for Education and Skills.

DfES (2002a) *Standards for Adventure* (DfES 0565 2002). London: Department for Education and Skills.

DfES (2002b) *Time for Standards* (Proposals DfES/0751/2002). London: Department for Education and Skills.

DfES (2003a) *Raising Standards and Tackling Workload*. London: Department for Education and Skills with Workforce Agreement Monitoring Group (WAMG).

DfES (2003b) *The Core Principles – Teaching and Learning School Improvement System Wide Reform* (Consultation). London: Department for Education and Skills.

DfES (2003c) *Excellence and Enjoyment: A Strategy for Primary Schools* (Advice DfES/0377/2003). London: Department for Education and Skills.

DfES (2004a) *Removing Barriers to Achievement* (DfES/0117/2004). London: Department for Education and Skills.

DfES (2004b) *Working Together – Giving Young People a Say* (DfES/0134/2004). London: Department of Education and Skills.

DfES (2004c) *Drugs Guidance for Schools* (DfES 0092 2004). London: Department for Education and Skills.

DfES (2004d) *Every Child Matters – The Next Steps*. London: Department for Education and Skills.

DfES (2004e) *Safeguarding Children in Education* (Guidance DfES/0027/2004). London: Department for Education and Skills.

DfES (2004f) *Role and Context Module: Induction Training for Teaching Assistants in Primary Schools*. London: Department for Education and Skills.

DfES (2004g) *Role and Context Module: Induction Training for Teaching Assistants in Secondary Schools*. London: Department for Education and Skills.

DfES (2004h) *Teaching Assistant File: Induction Training for Teaching Assistants in Primary Schools*. London: Department for Education and Skills.

DfES (2004i) *Teaching Assistant File: Induction Training for Teaching Assistants in Secondary Schools*. London: Department for Education and Skills.

DfES, Clarke, C., Boateng, P. and Hodge, M. (2003) *Every Child Matters* (Green Paper CYPUECM). London: Department for Education and Skills.

DfES, and Ofsted (2004) *A New Relationship with Schools* (PP/D16/(5585)/0604/22). London: Department for Education and Skills and Ofsted.

DfES and TTA (2003) *Professional Standards for Higher Level Teaching Assistants*. London: Departments for Education and Skills and the Teacher Training Agency.

DH, HO, DfES, dcms, ODPM and LC (2003) *What to Do if You're Worried that a Child is Being Abused* (31553). London: Department of Health, Home Office, Department of Education and Skills, Department for Culture, Media and Sport, Office of the Deputy Prime Minister and the Lord Chancellor.

Eaude, T. (2004) *Values Education: Developing Positive Attitudes*. Birmingham: National Primary Trust with Oxfordshire County Council.

Education Act 1998. Statutory instrument 2003 no. 1663 The Education (Specified work and registration) (England) Regulations 2003 (2003).

Elton, R. (1989) *Discipline in Schools* (Report of the Committee of Enquiry). London: Department of Education and the Welsh Office.

EO (2004) *Qualifications for Teaching Assistants* (Version 2). London: Employers' Organisation for Local Government.

Evans, G. (2004) 'Recent Issues and Controversies in English Education Policy', in Matheson, D. (ed.) *An Introduction to the Study of Education*, 2nd edn, pp. 262–77. London: David Fulton Publishers.

Formation (2004) Private Communications.

Freiberg, H. J. and Stein, T. A. (1999) 'Measuring, improving and sustaining healthy learning environments', in Freiberg H. J., (ed.) *School Climate*, pp. 11–29. London and Philadelphia: Falmer Press.

Fullan, M. and Hargreaves, A. (1992) *What's Worth Fighting for in Your School?* Buckingham: Open University Press in association with the Ontario Public School Teachers' Federation.

Gardner, H. (1983) *Frames of Mind: The Theory of Multiple Intelligences*. New York: Basic Books.

Goleman, D. (1996) *Emotional Intelligence*. London: Bloomsbury Publishing PLC.

GTC (2002) *Code of Professional Values and Practice for Teachers* [www.gtce.org.uk/gtcinfo/code.asp]. General Teaching Council for England.

Hargreaves, D. H. and Hopkins, D. (1991) *The Empowered School.* London: Cassell Education Limited.

Hastings, S. (2004) 'Emotional intelligence'. *Times Educational Supplement,* 15th October, pp. 11–14.

Hayes, D. (2000) *The Handbook for Newly Qualified Teachers – Meeting the Standards in Primary and Middle Schools.* London: David Fulton Publishers.

Hayes, D. (2003) *Planning, Teaching and Class Management in Primary Schools,* 2nd edn. London: David Fulton Publishers.

Hobby, R. (2004) *A Culture for Learning.* London: The Hay Group Management Ltd.

James, F. and Brownsword, K. (1994) *A Positive Approach.* Twickenham: Belair Publications Limited.

Lacey, P. (2001) *Support Partnerships.* London: David Fulton Publishers.

Leadbeater, C. (2004) *Learning About Personalisation: How Can We Put the Learner at the Heart of the Education System?* London: Department for Education and Skills in partnership with DEMOS and the National College for School Leadership.

LGNTO (2001) *Teaching/Classroom Assistants National Occupational Standards.* London: Local Government National Training Organisation.

LSC (2003) *Be Safe.* London: Learning and Skills Council.

MacBeath, J., Boyd, B. J. R. and Bell, S. (1996) *School Speak for Themselves.* National Union of Teachers for the University of Strathclyde.

MacGilchrist, B., Myers, K. and Reed, J. (2004) *The Intelligent School,* 2nd edn. London, Thousand Oaks and New Delhi: Sage.

Matheson, D. (2004) 'What is education?', in Matheson, D. (ed.) *An Introduction to a Study of Education,* 2nd edn, pp. 1–16. London: David Fulton Publishers.

Morris, E. (2001) *Professionalism and Trust* (speech to Social Market Foundation). London: Department for Education and Skills.

Mortimore, P., Sammons, P., Stoll, L., Lewis, D. and Ecob, R. (1988) *School Matters.* Wells: Open Books Publishing.

Mosley, J. (1993) *Turn Your School Round.* Wisbech: LDA.

NJC (2003) *Support Staff – The Way Forward.* London: Employers Organisation for the National Joint Council for Local Government Services.

O'Brien, T. and Garner, P. (2001) *Untold Stories – Learning Support Assistants and Their Work.* Stoke-on-Trent and Sterling: Trentham Books.

O'Flynn, S., Kennedy, H. and Macgrath, M. (2003) *Get Their Attention – How to Gain the Respect of Students and Thrive as a Teacher.* London: David Fulton Publishers.

Ofsted (2003) *Handbook for Inspecting Nursery and Primary Schools.* (May 2003 edn, Vol. HMI 1359). London: Office for Standards in Education.

Orlick, S. (2004) 'The professional framework and professional values and practice', in Brooks, V., Abbott, I. and Bills, L. (eds) *Preparing to Teach in Secondary Schools.* Maidenhead and New York: Open University Press.

Pollard, A. (2002a) *Reflective Teaching – Effective and Evidence-Informed Professional Practice.* London and New York: Continuum.

Pollard, A. (ed.) (2002b) *Readings for Reflective Teaching.* London and New York: Continuum.

Potts, S. (2004) 'Counselling and guidance in education', in Bold, C. (ed.) *Supporting Learning and Teaching.* London: David Fulton Publishers.

PricewaterhouseCoopers (2001) *Teacher Workload Study* (Draft final report). London: PricewaterhouseCoopers.

Ritchie, C. and Thomas, P. (2004) *Successful Study – Skills for Teaching Assistants.* London: David Fulton Publishers.

Rogers, B. (1991) *You Know the Fair Rule.* Harlow: Longman.

Rogers, B. (2000) *Classroom Behaviour.* London, Thousand Oaks and New Delhi: Paul Chapman Publishing (Sage).

Sammons, P. H. J. and Mortimore, P. (1995) *Key Characteristics of Effective Schools.* London: Office for Standards in Education.

Senge, P. M. (1990) *The Fifth Discipline.* London, Sydney, Auckland and Parktown SA: Century Business.

Senge, P. M., Cambron-McCabe, N., Lucas, T., Smith, B., Dutton, J. and Kleiner, A. (2000) *Schools that Learn.* London and Yarmouth, USA: Nicholas Brealey Publishing.

Silcock, P. (2003) 'Problems and prospects for primary school teacher-professionalism.' *Education 2,* 13, 31(2), pp. 26–33.

Smith, P., Whitby, K. and Sharp, S. (2004) *The Employment and Deployment of Teaching Assistants* (LGA 5/04). Slough: National Foundation for Educational research with the Local Government Association.

Stoll, L. and Fink, D. (1995) *Changing our Schools.* Buckingham and Philadelphia: Open University Press.

Thomas, G. W. D. and Webb, J. (1998) *The Making of the Inclusive School*. London and New York: Routledge.

TTA (2004) *Guidance to the Standards – Meeting the Professional Standards for the Award of Higher Level Teaching Assistants*. London: Teacher Training Agency.

Unison (2004) *School Support Staff Survey*. London: Unison.

Watkinson, A. (1999) 'The professional development of teaching assistants', in *Professional Development Today*, 2,3, pp. 63–69.

Watkinson, A. (2002) *Assisting Learning and Supporting Teaching*. London: David Fulton Publishers.

Watkinson, A. (2003a) *The Essential Guide for Competent Teaching Assistants – Meeting the National Occupational Standards at Level 2*. London: David Fulton Publishers.

Watkinson, A. (2003b) *The Essential Guide for Experienced Teaching Assistants – Meeting the National Occupational Standards at Level 3*. London: David Fulton Publishers.

Watkinson, A. (2003c) *Managing Teaching Assistants – A Guide for Headteachers, Managers and Teachers*. London: Routledge Falmer.

Wragg, E. C. (1994) *An Introduction to Classroom Observation*. London and New York. Routledge.

Index